Canaries in the Code Mine

MAX PAPADANTONAKIS

Canaries in the Code Mine

Precarity and the Future of Tech Work

TEMPLE UNIVERSITY PRESS
Philadelphia • Rome • Tokyo

TEMPLE UNIVERSITY PRESS
Philadelphia, Pennsylvania 19122
tupress.temple.edu

Library of Congress Cataloging-in-Publication Data

Names: Papadantonakis, Max, 1989– author.
Title: Canaries in the code mine : precarity and the future of tech work /
Max Papadantonakis.
Description: Philadelphia : Temple University Press, 2025. | Includes
bibliographical references and index. | Summary: "This book shows how
people who go into professional careers in technology, such as
programming and software development, have found the job security they
sought short-lived. Their difficulty finding and keeping work is
exacerbated if they do not fit the stereotype of the ideal tech worker:
young, male, and white"— Provided by publisher.
Identifiers: LCCN 2024062089 (print) | LCCN 2024062090 (ebook) | ISBN
9781439925775 (cloth) | ISBN 9781439925782 (paperback) | ISBN
9781439925799 (pdf)
Subjects: LCSH: High technology industries—Employees—Supply and
demand—United States. | High technology industries—Employees—Effect
of technological innovations on—United States. | Computer
industry—Employees—Supply and demand—United States. | Computer
industry—Employees—Effect of technological innovations on—United
States. | Discrimination in employment—United States.
Classification: LCC HD8039.H542 .P37 2025 (print) | LCC HD8039.H542
(ebook) | DDC 331.700973—dc23/eng/20250217
LC record available at https://lccn.loc.gov/2024062089
LC ebook record available at https://lccn.loc.gov/2024444455

The manufacturer's authorized representative in the EU for product safety
is Temple University Rome, Via di San Sebastianello, 16, 00187 Rome RM,
Italy (https://rome.temple.edu/).
tempress@temple.edu

Printed in the United States of America

9 8 7 6 5 4 3 2 1

In memory of William (Bill) Helmreich

Contents

Preface

In March 2024, I boarded a flight to San Francisco from New York for a job interview. Once seated, I began reviewing my talk on precarious work among software developers. Soon, the man and woman seated next to me struck up a conversation about a topic that now slips my mind. Eventually, we introduced ourselves. It felt almost like an omen when they revealed their professions: the man was a software developer on a business trip to San Francisco, and the woman was a former software developer who had transitioned into law, specializing in discrimination cases.

Let's refer to the man as Lars. Lars shared how stressful his work life had been, constantly tackling new projects to stay current and facing significant insecurity from frequent job changes. Despite landing a job at a prestigious company during the COVID-19 pandemic, thinking he had found stability, he was laid off last year in the initial round of cutbacks. Lars, a thirty-five-year-old white man recognizes his privileged position within the tech industry, which gives him certain advantages. Nonetheless, Lars sees himself as a precarious worker. Over the next hours he went on to describe how working as a software developer can be exceptionally draining, expressing relief that someone was writing a book on the subject. He shared that many of his coworkers felt the same way, grappling with the relentless pace and high demands of the industry and balancing on a very thin tight rope that can snap at any moment, despite earning high salaries.[1]

Seated next to Lars was a woman in her seventies, whom we'll refer to as Melissa. Melissa had embarked on a career in software development in her twenties but chose to leave the field due to the discrimination she faced. This pivotal experience led her to pursue a career in law, focusing on discrimination lawsuits. Despite being a woman in the male-dominated software development industry, Melissa enjoyed the problem-solving aspect of her work. However, she found the work environment untenable. She enjoyed the intellectual challenge of software development, but the pervasive "boys' club" atmosphere made it impossible for her to continue. Melissa was not willing to endure that just to do what she loved.

I begin my book with this recent experience to emphasize some of the continuities and new developments we see in the tech industry. Melissa embodies the enduring disparities that have characterized the industry from its inception. Conversely, Lars symbolizes the contemporary challenges this book also aims to address: a widespread precarity marked by job insecurity, uncertainty, anxiety, and imposter syndrome. These problems persist, affecting all workers despite the generally high salaries.

This paradox became apparent to me early in my research, particularly during initial interviews conducted at hackathons, where I collaborated with Sharon Zukin on our study of New York City's tech ecosystem. During weekends, I visited multiple hackathons—forty-eight-hour coding competitions held throughout New York City. My goal was to unravel how participants perceived these events. What drives them to engage in these intense, time-constrained challenges? Is it purely for enjoyment, or do they benefit from their participation?

Once I began my interviews, it became clear that many attended these events on their weekends, after enduring long workweeks, with the aim of advancing their careers. They sought to build connections, win prizes, interact with recruiters, while at the same time enjoy coding alongside both old and new friends. Yet the question that intrigued me was, "Why would you spend your weekend doing this?" This question was especially perplexing when considering participants who worked for high-profile companies such as Google or JP Morgan, earning salaries that reached and surpassed $200,000 a year. It seemed counterintuitive. As I talked to more people, I stumbled upon the theme that would captivate me for the next eight years.

Precarity among software developers is about more than just job security. Even those with high-paying positions at top companies face uncertainties. Many software developers are on temporary contracts without stable benefits, creating a constant worry about what comes next. There's the threat of sudden job loss due to project cancellations and company downsizing. In addition, a significant number of these professionals are tied to their employers due to the H-1B immigrant visa, which complicates their employment stability further, as their ability to stay in the job and the country is contingent on their employment status. Beyond the workplace, this instability affects their lives significantly.

Despite earning good salaries, many software developers live with a pervasive anxiety about the future, feeling that no matter how well they are doing, it is never quite secure enough. This underlying fear can make them hesitant to commit to long-term financial obligations such as buying a house or maintaining consistent health-care coverage. The high stakes of their positions, coupled with the rapid advancements in technology such as artificial intelligence (AI), add to this uncertainty, reinforcing their sense of vulnerability even at the top of their careers. The transient nature of tech jobs can hinder forming lasting community ties or feeling a sense of belonging in one place. Such isolation influences not just their current living conditions but also their future security and personal life stability, creating a constant state of alertness about potential downturns or shifts in their professional and personal lives.

This pervasive anxiety experienced by software developers is part of a broader phenomenon known as precarity. Precarity captures the nuances of insecure employment and extends to a wider sense of existential precariousness, affecting various aspects of individual and collective life. This dual nature highlights not only the instability associated with jobs—such as temporary contracts, lack of benefits, and the constant threat of unemployment—but also a more pervasive sense of vulnerability that permeates life beyond the workplace. Precarity is not just about the risk of losing one's job; it is about living in a state where basic needs and rights are not guaranteed. It touches upon the fundamental aspects of living a dignified life, including access to health care, housing, and social security, as well as mutual respect, recognition, and belonging.[2]

To write this book I engaged with various communities, attending meetups and events prior to the COVID-19 pandemic. When the world shifted online due to the pandemic, I continued my research online and connected with software developers willing to share their experiences. This approach allowed me to gain a deeper understanding of the multifaceted nature of precarity, highlighting the significant roles that race, gender, and age play in shaping individuals' experiences of instability and vulnerability. I am profoundly thankful to all the respondents who opened up about some of the most challenging and painful moments of their careers. Their candidness enabled me to uncover the diverse manifestations of precarity, emphasizing the importance of recognizing these differences to fully comprehend inequality from every possible angle.[3]

The individuals whose stories I share in this work symbolize the "canaries in the code mine." Just as canaries once signaled danger in coal mines, these workers' experiences alert us to the perils of unchecked growth. Their narratives illuminate how this relentless expansion is underpinned by work that demands the sacrifice of workers' well-being and perpetuates the exploitation of women, racial minorities, and senior workers.

However, these stories are not just tales of individual and collective hardship but are indicative of systemic issues that necessitate a reevaluation of how technological progress is achieved. I hope this book will challenge readers to consider the human cost of innovation and to question the sustainability of a model that relies on the erosion of worker security and dignity. I hope to inspire you to think about how we can create a tech industry that advances without compromising the well-being of those who power its engines. This pursuit for a fairer and more just technological future involves redefining solidarity in the digital labor era and recognizing that, despite our differences, we find commonality in our shared precarity.

Acknowledgments

First and foremost, I am indebted to my informants and interviewees who sat down with me in noisy cafes before the pandemic and later on Zoom to answer my questions and suggest more people to interview. I greatly appreciate your openness and willingness to share your experiences with me. I hope that I have done a satisfactory job of retelling your stories and making sense of them in my book.

I finished this manuscript while working as an adjunct assistant professor at the City University of New York, School of Professional Studies, where Bonnie Oglensky and Regina Bernard offered their support during some very difficult times. I thank them for this, and I am ever so grateful.

My editor, Ryan Mulligan, believed in this project even before a single word was ever written on paper when it was merely a collection of abstract concepts. Your support, encouragement, and patience, especially during the final miles, meant the world to me. Thank you also to everyone else at Temple who made this a smooth project.

As a doctoral student at the City University of New York, I benefited from the expertise and guidance of my dissertation committee members: Thomas DeGloma, Richard Ocejo, Van Tran, and Steven Vallas. I am most grateful to my doctoral advisor, Sharon Zukin, who provided me with encouragement and intellectual support and gave me the freedom to grow as a researcher, writer, and scholar. Her insightful critiques and unwavering dedication to pushing the boundaries of my work have profoundly shaped my approach to academia. Sharon's mentorship instilled in me a deeper passion for exploring the complexities of social dynamics and addressing the contradictions inherent in social life.

I want to extend my thanks to all the members of the dissertation writing group: Viktor Bensus, Joanna Dressel, Ivana Mellers, Nga Than, Sebastián Villamizar-Santamaria, and Xiaohua Zhong, who were patient enough to read and comment on my work every month for the past three years. Your constructive criticism pushed me to become a better writer and grow as a thinker.

While at the Graduate Center, my work was supported by the Hendrik Muller Foundation Scholarship, Graduate Center Fellowship, Dissertation Writing Award, and a New York Connect Fellowship. I owe a debt of gratitude to Robert Hatcher and Jeff Erbe, who offered their support when I was overwhelmed with my studies and city life. I remain grateful to the Graduate Center's Sociology Department, especially Lynn Chancer, Rati Kashyap, and Phil Kasinitz, for their backing. I also thank Edwin Grimsley and Joseph van der Naald for their support and camaraderie.

I thank my family for their unwavering support and my friends for cheering me on. Last but not least, thank you to our cat, Dobby, who never let me write a single word without demanding attention, and to my wife, Alyse, who stood by me through thick and thin, gave me the courage to keep writing, suggested other books for inspiration, and helped me make this book a reality.

This book is dedicated to William Helmreich, with whom I took my first class, "The People of New York City," when I arrived in New York City in the summer of 2015. Bill taught me to be a better ethnographer, to just talk to people and not to be afraid of observing the most minute, banal things. During my dissertation proposal defense, he told me that this was going to be a book he wanted to read. Thank you, Bill, for all your support; you are truly missed.

Canaries in the Code Mine

Introduction

Sam, a thirty-six-year-old software developer, epitomizes the typical demographic in the tech industry, characterized by young, unmarried, white male professionals. His career features a series of brief tenures at various start-ups, which have provided opportunities for higher salaries, stock compensation, connections, and exposure to niche technologies. Facilitating his career, Sam had the support of several mentors—veteran figures in the industry with similar social and educational backgrounds who gave him access to an influential network and smoothed his career path.

In 2020, amid the instability caused by the COVID-19 pandemic, Sam saw opportunity. The shift toward digital services spiked the demand for software developers. Sam upgraded his skills and leveraged this demand to negotiate better salaries and frequent job transitions, positioning himself advantageously within the sector. In early 2023, as the tech industry faced post-pandemic challenges such as overexpansion and layoffs, Sam's career trajectory was unaffected. Unlike many peers who were losing their jobs, Sam had made strategic choices during the pandemic that ensured he remained sought after in the industry.

While Sam's job-hopping allowed him to thrive early in his career, it exacted a cost. At thirty-six, nearing the age considered "too old" to code, Sam hit a roadblock. His daily life dissolved into a blur of nonstop coding, with eighty-hour workweeks becoming the norm. This relentless schedule was fueled partly by fear that he would be perceived as less capable due to his age and partly by his desire to continually prove his productivity and learn new skills. With an ironic twist in his tone, Sam noted, "I survived several 'crashes,' but not my own." Recognizing this, Sam chose to step away from software development and working in tech.[1]

Emma, a twenty-seven-year-old white woman with a degree in computer science, started her career filled with aspirations. She interned at a leading tech company during her final year of college and joined it as a full-time employee after graduation, eager to dive deep into software development with a long-term goal of specializing in software architecture. However, two years in as a junior software developer, Emma observed a troubling pattern: Despite her capabilities and dedication, she was frequently diverted from core development tasks to software testing, a field often marked by gender biases. She noticed that her male colleagues with equivalent experience were consistently assigned more complex coding projects.

Despite her reservations, Emma decided to heed her manager's advice to persevere for another year, hoping it would lead to greater responsibilities. Yet a year later, at her assessment, she faced a stark change: Her once supportive manager had left the company, and the new management viewed her role differently. They offered her a position as a software tester with a significant raise, framing it as a "natural progression" and a testament to her "inherent talent" for the role. This new position would also mean relocating within the company, distancing her from her current team. Faced with this unexpected turn, Emma was left to choose between accepting the new role or seeking opportunities elsewhere.

But then the COVID-19 pandemic happened. Emma chose to remain in her testing role, despite growing dissatisfaction with her career trajectory, influenced by the adverse experiences of other women navigating the job market in these uncertain times. To make matters worse, her role as a tester was often trivialized, bearing the brunt of gendered stereotypes. Her crucial testing work was belittled as mere "cleaning up" after the "real" work done by male developers. Although she eventually led a team of testers, the persistent stereotype of testers as the "cleaners" among "builders" created a barrier to her hope to become a software architect—a barrier that she could not cross.

Diana, a Black woman, is the same age as Emma. She started her career in a similar fashion, graduating from college with a computer science degree. After graduation she secured a temporary position with a well-known tech company. However, after six months Diana observed that her predominantly white peers were moving effortlessly into full-time positions, complete with benefits such as health insurance, vacation time, and access to free office meals. Meanwhile, Diana continued as a contract worker, earning considerably less and missing out on the stability and security her full-time colleagues had.

Diana's and Emma's careers have similarities. Both faced marginalization as women; however, Diana encountered additional layers of racial bias. She frequently encountered prejudice from her predominantly white male coworkers. They would habitually question her capabilities, make negative assumptions based on her gender, and confuse her with the few other Black employees in the office. On more than one occasion, she was stopped and asked, "Do you work here?" an inquiry that not only underscored her perceived inferior professional status but also singled her out as a racial outsider.

Amid these challenges, Diana found it particularly difficult to secure a mentor within the company—a key rung to climb on the software developer ladder. Although many of her white colleagues were quickly paired with experienced developers who provided guidance and networking opportunities, Diana faced isolation. Her attempts to connect with potential mentors were often met with polite deflections or, worse, indifference. The absence of mentorship meant that Diana struggled to navigate the often unwritten rules of advancement in the tech world, further stymieing her progression within the company.

In an effort to navigate the challenges she faced at work, Diana turned to external networks, joining online workshops and seminars tailored specifically for Black and Latine software developers. But these platforms, while providing essential emotional support and a sense of empowerment, did little to shield her from poor working conditions. The end of her contract with her initial employer was particularly hard-hitting, due especially to the company's stringent policy that prohibited reapplication for two years. This forced her into a tumultuous job search, which resulted only in successive contract positions and a relentless mix of burnout, microaggressions, and job insecurity.

Kareem, a forty-eight-year-old Black software developer, faced challenges early in his life. Growing up with a single mother and two siblings in financially constrained circumstances, he was fortunate to receive a scholarship to study computer science. Before getting the scholarship, Kareem made use of the computers at his local public library, teaching himself web design. With a touch of nostalgia, he shared that what was once a mere hobby was regarded as a prized skill in those days.

After obtaining his degree in computer science, Kareem worked in finance for several years, helping to computerize the trade system that brokers used. His career faced a sudden halt during the financial crisis of 2008. Yet by early 2010, even as many companies still grappled with the aftermath of the crisis, Kareem began receiving job offers. In one of his roles, he worked closely with a team of software developers on a project designed to assist opiate users in securely obtaining their prescription medication from pharmacies, police stations, and other designated locations. The primary goal of the initiative was to ensure that only people with valid prescriptions could access these medications, thereby reducing the risk of unauthorized use and helping to prevent addiction.

Despite his achievements, Kareem confronted roadblocks that went beyond mere technical challenges. As an almost fifty-year-old Black man in a largely white-dominated sector, he grappled with the intersections of racial prejudice and age discrimination. His deep reservoir of knowledge and extensive experience often found no acknowledgment. Younger colleagues, and often those in managerial positions, perceived him as "stubborn," casting his insights aside. When Kareem took the initiative, proposing improvements or strategic changes, he was met with hesitation: His white peers seemed unprepared, perhaps even unwilling, to acknowledge a Black man's authority and expertise.

At forty-eight, Kareem feels out of place in the tech industry. While his race plays a role, his age stands out as an equally prominent barrier. Consequently, he's shifted his focus to freelancing on platforms such as Upwork, where he competes with software developers in other regions of the world who often charge significantly less than he does. Every six months, Kareem aims to develop two to three products, each crafted with the hope of generating a consistent income. In the face of persistent challenges, his story embodies a stark reality: Even with talent and experience, navigating racial and age biases remains a daunting task.

Renowned for its innovation and transformative impact, the tech sector also serves as a prime example of modern labor's precarious nature. Software developers, despite their technical expertise, high salaries, and crucial roles in product innovation, find their experiences marked by precarity, resembling those of gig economy workers more than the stable corporate elite. As the four stories described earlier illustrate, precarity within the industry is intensified by systemic inequalities. Race, gender, and age significantly influence an individual's perceived value in a sector that traditionally privileges whiteness, masculinity, and youth. These dynamics generate a spectrum of experiences within the digital economy's unstable labor market, where only a privileged few can navigate uncertainty.

The Myth of Progress

On the surface, the tech industry does not reveal precarity. Many workers enter it with hope that it offers greater security than the industries it disrupts. Corporations such as Apple, Google, Meta, Microsoft, and Amazon lead the way in cutting-edge products that dominate global markets. At the heart of these innovations are software developers, who possess the technical expertise to design and build pioneering technologies, making them what the economist David Autor calls "frontier workers" in the twenty-first-century economy.[2] These workers are in high demand with companies both within and beyond the tech industry. Not only do they possess the skills to write complex computer code, but they are also creative problem solvers who drive innovation. The median salary for software developers—$130,160 per year—not only reflects their individual value but emphasizes the recognition of technical skills as a gateway to transformative opportunities in our tech-centric society.[3]

During the global pandemic, the sudden shift to working from home and the demand for new technologies bolstered the power of the tech industry. In this new landscape, the most sought-after professionals—software developers—experienced a notable increase in their value. Their expertise became critically important, as they were urgently needed to assist organizations in transitioning to online platforms and expanding their digital infrastructures. For many businesses, software developers emerged as indispensable. Some even went as far as describing their jobs as recession-proof, reflecting the increased reliance on technology in almost every aspect of modern life.[4]

These trends might lead an observer to assume that software developers should not have concerns about the future. Yet many do. Despite high salaries, software developers face precarious work conditions due to several key factors. As companies strive to reduce costs, stable career prospects have significantly deteriorated. This includes adopting temporary work contracts and a flexible division of labor, challenging workers' employability and career stability. In addition, a shift toward centralizing production decisions has reduced the autonomy and creative input of individual teams and developers, leading to stricter labor control and cost-cutting measures. Furthermore, the tech industry's reliance on a global labor market, with increasing use of outsourcing and hiring immigrant workers from regions with lower labor costs, intensifies competition and the use of temporary contracts, reflecting the industry's continuously evolving labor practices in a highly competitive market.[5]

Traditionally, professions such as software development offered significant job security. However, the increasing prevalence of contract-based work within these high-paying sectors points to a pivotal shift away from stable, permanent employment models. This change is largely driven by employers' pursuit of greater flexibility and their aim to minimize costs linked to long-term commitments to employees, such as pensions and health-care benefits. The evolving landscape in software development underscores a broader trend: In today's high-technology job market, fluid employment terms have become the standard, and the concept of job security is becoming increasingly obsolete, even among the most skilled workers.[6]

The advent of the gig economy, exemplified by companies such as Uber recruiting labor for on-demand tasks, has also contributed to an increase in job insecurity, shifting away from long-term employment commitments toward corporate adaptability. This trend, driven by digitalization, has reshaped the labor market into one dominated by short-term engagements, mediated by platforms such as Upwork, which offers individuals flexibility in their work schedules but at the cost of traditional employment benefits such as health insurance, paid leave, and retirement savings. Consequently, there has been a significant shift toward more fluid work arrangements such as freelance, contractual, and temporary positions. Tech companies, adapting their workforce to the varying demands of production stages, hire people for in-demand technical skills and release those with less relevant abilities, leading to a core-periphery structure within many organizations. A small number of full-time employees hold high-earning, prestigious positions, while a larger group of workers occupies lower-paying, temporary roles.[7]

The organizational structure of tech companies also affects the quality of jobs. Large companies such as Google often feature traditional hierarchical structures with multiple levels of management, providing employees with various career opportunities. This contrasts with many start-ups and small firms that adopt a flat organizational structure, characterized by an antibureaucratic approach and fewer management layers. Such flat structures can limit internal career advancement, driving workers to seek career growth and salary increases externally. Furthermore, start-ups are infamous for their instability, largely stemming from reliance on attracting venture capital. These firms constantly adapt to their investors' demands—sometimes demands to expand, and at other times pressure to cut back and cut costs. This leads to minimal job security and frequent organizational changes, including job cuts.[8]

The unpredictable nature of the tech industry leads professionals to approach their careers with a strategy similar to managing investments. This perspective does not view employment as a literal financial investment but, rather, recognizes that career opportunities can fluctuate significantly. Consequently, professionals often plan their career paths with a focus on frequent company changes, aiming to build financial security, enhance their personal brands, and strengthen their professional networks, much as investors diversify and manage their portfolios to maximize returns and mitigate risks.[9]

But what makes tech different from other sectors, such as finance and architecture, where these changes have also been described? The tech industry experiences a more rapid pace of technological change. In a span of a mere decade, the cutting-edge tools software developers once mastered can become relics of the past. For example, TikTok became a global sensation in 2020, especially among Gen Z, for its short-form video content. Its rapid success led major platforms such as Instagram and YouTube to introduce similar features, Reels and Shorts, respectively. This swift rise showcases the speed of digital trends in today's digital era. The dynamic nature of the software field means that staying stationary isn't an option. A year of complacency can render an individual developer's knowledge outdated. In a span of a few years, one might find oneself a relic of a bygone technological era.[10]

Software developers face another emerging threat: Advancements in artificial intelligence (AI) are fundamentally altering the nature of work. GitHub's Copilot, which is powered by OpenAI's Codex, and other AI-driven tools are automating tasks that traditionally were completed by software developers, such as code generation and debugging. This automation extends to software testing and quality assurance, where AI technologies automate test case writing and execution, roles that once required significant human effort. Such developments underscore a profound irony: As software developers strive to push the boundaries of technology and efficiency, they may be unwittingly paving the way for a future in which their expertise is less sought after or, in extreme cases, no longer needed.[11]

Canaries in the Code Mine

Historically, canaries were used in coal mines to detect the presence of toxic gases, serving as early warning systems for miners. This role finds a contemporary parallel in the experiences of software developers in the tech industry. Regarded as the industry's most prized workers, software developers are now encountering job instability, contract work without benefits, and the constant threat of layoffs due to project cancellations, company downsizing, and advancements in AI. This precariousness challenges the notion of the tech sector as a stable and secure employment realm. It suggests that the vulnerabilities faced by these workers are indicative of broader economic shifts that impact the middle class at large.

Increasingly, high-skilled professions are facing precarious work conditions. Traditionally shielded by professional qualifications and stable jobs, high-skilled software developers now find their protections eroding. This shift exposes a broader swath of the workforce to economic instability, a condition once primarily confined to lower-skilled jobs. In his book *Good Jobs, Bad Jobs*, Arne Kalleberg explores how the quality of employment has deteriorated over time, highlighting the rise of precarious work even among traditionally secure professions. He argues that the labor market has become increasingly polarized, with fewer "good jobs" that offer stability, benefits, and decent wages, and more "bad jobs" that are insecure and low paid and lack benefits. Software developers are signaling that we are entering an era in which high wages no longer equate to job security, fundamentally altering the social contract that has underpinned middle-class economic stability in the postwar period.[12]

Software developers, in facing these challenges, serve as harbingers of broader economic shifts. Their experiences highlight deep structural changes in labor markets, driven by technological advancement and neoliberal policies that favor labor flexibility over security. Consequently, the plight of software developers may well prefigure future challenges for the broader workforce, making their experiences critical for understanding the evolving landscape of work and economic security in the twenty-first century. Enter the digital precariat.

Digital Precariat

The differentiation in job security and benefits within the tech industry underscores growing inequalities within this professional class.
While a select few workers secure lucrative, stable positions, a vast
majority face precarious employment scenarios akin to gig work. This
dynamic is creating a stark stratification within the tech industry,
where a small number of digital elites enjoy substantial security and
benefits while a large pool of digital workers endures instability and
uncertainty. This stratification is not random; it is deeply influenced
by race, gender, and age. Senior software developers, women, and
people of color are disproportionately represented in the precarious
segment of the workforce, often relegated to contract work with few to
no benefits. Meanwhile, younger white male software developers are
more likely to hold the secure, high-paying positions. The rise of the
digital precariat signals a future in which high-skilled work does not
guarantee stability and exacerbates existing social divisions.[13]

Building on this understanding, *Canaries in the Code Mine* ex-
pands the discussion of the digital precariat to acknowledge both
the class nuances and the diversity within this new labor category.
For the privileged, precarious work becomes a stepping stone for career advancement. These individuals, typically young white or Asian
men, embody the ideal tech worker: adaptable, entrepreneurial, and
resilient in the face of changing projects and contracts. Their success
stems not just from their abilities but, significantly, also from their
social status, positioning them advantageously within the upper echelons of the tech hierarchy. Enjoying lucrative salaries and elevated
status, they leverage this privilege for greater flexibility in their careers, choosing projects and shaping their work paths. For them, the
industry's unpredictability is not a hindrance but a landscape that is
rich in opportunities.[14]

In stark contrast to their privileged counterparts, women, people
of color, and senior employees are more frequently found in roles
characterized by temporary contracts, lower wages, and diminished
opportunities for advancement. Moreover, their positions are often affected first during layoffs and are increasingly vulnerable to displace-

ment by advancements in AI. These employees are more vulnerable to the industry's inherent precarity while also having to deal with a hostile work environment that does not equally distribute opportunities for advancement.[15]

Tech companies heavily rely on contract workers to reduce labor costs, enhance operational flexibility, and meet production needs, to the extent that contract employees now outnumber full-time employees. This preference is visible if one visits any Google office: Contract employees identified by red badges flood the company's common spaces, while full-time employees wearing green badges are harder to spot.[16] The increasing reliance on temporary workers, particularly among software developers, thrusts workers into a state of professional uncertainty, affecting not just job security but also access to crucial career development resources such as mentorship. This trend disproportionately impacts women and people of color, who are more likely to be hired into these roles and experience pay disparities and lack of benefits.[17]

In 2023, following three years of pandemic-induced growth, Twitter and Facebook announced significant workforce reductions, with many other companies quickly following suit. Twitter, under new ownership, laid off about half of its employees, aiming to streamline operations and cut costs. Facebook's parent company, Meta, announced a reduction of thousands of jobs, particularly targeting contract work and diversity, equity, and inclusion (DEI) positions, marking the company's first significant layoffs since its inception. These layoffs sent ripples through the industry, prompting workers to reassess their career stability and future within the sector.[18]

The challenges just described are significantly intensified by the enduring effects of toxic workplace environments, which have been exacerbated by the shift to remote work. For instance, the use of productivity tools in remote settings has opened new avenues for workplace toxicity, from bullying during group video calls to the sharing of racist and sexist content in chat software. In addition, while remote work has offered greater geographic flexibility and protection from pandemic-related risks, it has also led to increased anxiety and longer working hours for many. These conditions not only undermine the daily work experience; they also contribute to a growing sense of isolation and alienation among employees. Such toxicity frequently arises from, and is magnified by, intersecting inequalities related to gender, race, and age, thereby disproportionately affecting the most vulnerable workers. Together, these elements foster an environment in which work is not only a source of employment uncertainty but also a realm fraught with social and psychological challenges.[19]

But collective action has not been widespread, despite the glaring inequalities and precarities. A compelling professional ethos has emerged, rooted in a powerful narrative of innovation, opportunity, and meritocracy, that continues to draw people to the tech industry. The allure lies in the promise of being at the forefront of technological advancement, the potential for significant financial gain, and the chance to be part of a field that shapes the future. This narrative is reinforced by high-profile success stories of tech entrepreneurs and software developers who have risen to fame and fortune, further perpetuating the belief that anyone with talent and determination can achieve similar success. The dominance of this professional ethos makes collective action challenging. The highly individualized nature of career advancement in tech, coupled with the competitive atmosphere, often discourages workers from banding together to demand better conditions. Efforts to unionize or advocate for systemic changes are frequently met with resistance, both from within the workforce and from industry leaders who benefit from maintaining the status quo.

The Myth of Meritocracy

As unique as the tech industry is in its embrace of the future, its guiding philosophies are not so far removed from those of other middle-class professions that look to its lessons. So the trends pioneered in tech work and the precarities afflicting the middle class of that industry are worth looking at for clues about the future of professional culture more broadly.

Tech companies, particularly in hubs such as Silicon Valley, epitomize a powerful belief: the meritocratic promise. At the core of this ideal lies the conviction that anyone, regardless of social background or social standing, can ascend the professional ladder through sheer talent, determination, and hard work. An example of this can be found in the story of Jan Koum, who immigrated to the United States from Ukraine with his mother in 1992, when he was sixteen. They settled in Mountain View, California, where they struggled financially, relying on food stamps and government assistance. Despite these challenges, Koum developed a passion for programming and taught himself how to write computer code. Eventually he was hired by Yahoo. After working with the company for nearly a decade, he went on to cofound WhatsApp, a company that was eventually sold to Facebook for $19 billion.[20]

In cities with diverse, low-income populations, such as New York, the meritocratic narrative offers something more. It's an invitation that echoes, "With hard work, perseverance, and the right skills, you can move from disadvantage to a high-paying tech job." This narrative has transformed tech work into a symbol of social mobility. One example of this in action is the New York City Tech Talent Pipeline, a collaboration among the city, educational institutions, and tech industry. The collaboration asserts that, since 2014, its targeted training and mentorship programs have connected thousands of New Yorkers from diverse and low-income backgrounds to lucrative careers. The focus on building bridges between underserved communities and the tech industry aims to redefine what it means to work in tech, offering opportunities for those who have the determination and the technical skills to seize them.[21]

Strengthening the meritocratic promise is the tech industry's repeated assertions that coding capabilities are primary indicators of success. The hiring and promotion of top candidates, known as "tech talent," are perceived to hinge on an objective evaluation of their proficiency in programming and their knack for solving intricate technical problems. Writing exceptional computer code epitomizes the meritocratic essence of a widely celebrated "hacker culture." Within this realm, self-taught coders can rival, if not surpass, their highly educated colleagues with advanced degrees in computer science.[22]

In an era when insecure employment has become widespread, the tech industry also places a premium on workers' adaptability. It is not just about who possesses a vast repository of technical skills; it is also about who can swiftly navigate and adjust to relentless change. This adaptability manifests in multiple forms. It could be acclimating to cutting-edge technologies that emerge almost daily; welcoming and integrating innovative business strategies; or even stepping up to address and navigate sudden, widespread global disruptions such as the onslaught of the COVID-19 pandemic. In this fast-paced era, adaptability doesn't just symbolize a mere quality; it has ascended to a level at which it's considered an invaluable asset, setting the "talented" apart from the rest.[23]

The dynamic of frequently switching jobs, which in past eras and in many industries was met with skepticism and often seen as a lack of commitment, has now evolved to symbolize the essence of the tech industry. Moving from one job to another isn't just a calculated career move; it's a testament to one's ability to embrace uncertainty and navigate change. The fluidity in career paths is powerfully captured by Reid Hoffman, the cofounder and executive chairman of LinkedIn, who proposes the analogy of careers resembling "tours of duty."[24] This perspective illuminates the contemporary, agile, and temporary nature of tech jobs yet underlines the intentionality and purpose behind each move. Consider a software developer who has worked for various start-ups, constantly shifting terrains and amassing a range of experiences. Her professional trajectory may now be perceived as an asset. In comparison, a software developer who has opted for a linear path, staying for many years within one company, might be viewed as less versatile. The underlying sentiment is that breadth of experience, coupled with the ability to adapt, is increasingly becoming a standard in evaluating professional value.[25]

The emphasis on individualism and continuous innovation, originating in small start-ups that prized agility and personal accountability over collective action, has transformed into an entrenched work ethos. Workers often internalize the belief that adaptation and skill acquisition are essential for individual success, rather than depending on collective bargaining for job security. This individualistic perspective reinforces the illusion that the tech industry is a purely merit-based system, masking existing inequalities and diminishing the value of collaborative efforts in creating a stable work environment.

Consequently, when faced with industry downturns or organizational changes, many employees in the industry experience a sense of isolation and insecurity.[26]

However, as the tech industry's myth of meritocracy unravels, so does the resistance to collective action. Increasing awareness of the systemic inequalities and precarity tech workers face is sparking a movement toward unionization and collective bargaining. Despite the entrenched culture of individualism and the significant pushback from industry leaders, there are growing calls for tech workers to unite and advocate for better working conditions, job security, and equitable treatment. For example, the successful unionization efforts at companies such as Google and Amazon, though still limited, represent a significant shift in the tech industry's labor dynamics.

Overview

In *Canaries in the Code Mine*, the stories and experiences of 120 software developers provide a vital perspective on the themes of privilege and vulnerability within the tech industry. Their diverse narratives counter the prevailing perception of a uniformly progressive and affluent economic sector. Instead, they highlight a reality in which advancements and innovations, often seen as hallmarks of progress, deepen societal divisions. These testimonies underscore an emerging archetype of the precarious tech worker, not only in the current economy, but as a likely fixture in the future.[27]

The book engages in a critical discourse on the evolving nature of work in the digital era, emphasizing the need for a more comprehensive understanding of the multifaceted challenges faced by all workers. It calls for a reevaluation of work in the context of ongoing digital transformations, advocating for policies and practices that recognize and address the disparities brought about by technological progress. In doing so, it contributes to the broader conversation about how to navigate and shape an equitable future in the rapidly evolving landscape of the tech industry.

Chapter 1, "Tech Talent and the Ideal Worker," delves into the evolution of the tech industry, tracing its journey from an early stage dominated by white male specialists to the present, where the work-force, although making strides toward diversity, is still characterized by deep-seated gender, racial, and age-based inequalities. The chapter critically assesses how Silicon Valley's emergence and the rise of "brogrammer" culture have reinforced enduring stereotypes, impacting the recognition of "tech talent" and influencing the dynamics of modern tech workplaces. In addition, it discusses recent discrimination lawsuits and diversity initiatives, examining their effectiveness and limitations in addressing these systemic issues.

Chapter 2, "Digital Elites," examines the advantageous standing of young white and Asian men. It opens with an overview of how these workers adopt ideologies centered on meritocracy, individualism, and entrepreneurship. The chapter then turns to their career strategies, such as networking, job-hopping, and personal branding, which are employed to transform precarious situations into opportunities. The chapter concludes by discussing how these workers rationalize their career approaches, linking them to their passion for technology and innovation.

Chapter 3, "Pretty Colors and Cleaning Up," focuses on the persistence of male-dominated spaces in large tech companies, despite efforts to achieve diversity. The chapter highlights how women in software development—specifically, those in roles such as front-end development and software testing—are often relegated to more precarious job positions. It concludes with an analysis of how diversity initiatives, while they may improve women's representation in technical fields, fall short of addressing the broader issue of gendered experiences in precarious employment.

Chapter 4, "'Excuse Me! Do You Work Here?'" explores the complex layers of inequality that disproportionately affect Black men and women in software development roles. The chapter focuses on how organizational policies and practices contribute to unequal distribution of resources such as job opportunities, wages, mentorship, and training programs, thereby perpetuating racial hierarchies among employees. The chapter concludes with an in-depth analysis of the interpersonal challenges and barriers that Black and Latine software professionals encounter in their careers.

Chapter 5, "'Too Old' to Code," investigates the marginalization of senior software developers within a culture that predominantly values youth and typically envisions the "ideal worker" as young, male, and white. The chapter begins by exploring the stereotypes surrounding senior workers, who are often perceived as slow, less productive, and resistant to change. These biases not only intensify their daily experience of precarity but also intertwine with gendered and racialized prejudices. The chapter highlights how senior workers, depending on their individual sociopolitical backgrounds, face a variety of challenges and precarities, which manifest in multiple, intersecting forms.

Chapter 6, "Tech Workers Unite!" critically examines both past and present attempts at unionization, dissecting the factors that have led to their successes and failures. Drawing on historical examples of successful labor movements and examining contemporary efforts within the tech industry, a roadmap will be outlined for tech workers to build a more just and equitable future.

1

Tech Talent and the Ideal Worker

For many software developers, securing a position at a tech company signifies the pinnacle of career achievement. Tech firms not only offer higher salaries than other industries but also provide a plethora of perks, including the option for remote work, flexible working hours, health benefits, generous parental leave policies, and retirement savings plans. Employees often have access to on-site amenities such as gyms, cafeterias serving nutritious meals, and relaxation areas. Many companies also offer stock options or equity, giving employees a stake in the company's success. Jobs at these companies are often touted as the "jobs of the future" and are seen as magnets for people for whom the tech industry has coined the term *tech talent*.

As an industry buzzword, *tech talent* refers to individuals who possess specialized skills in technology-related fields, such as software development, data science, and artificial intelligence (AI). Yet the term often embodies a combination of hard technical skills and soft skills. For instance, a software developer might excel not only in writing computer code but also in problem solving, teamwork, and innovative thinking. Workers recognized as tech talent not only embody the spirit of continuous learning but also demonstrate an eagerness to stay updated with the fast-paced evolution of technology, consistently keeping abreast of the latest technological tools and coding languages.[1]

The rise of tech talent marks a significant shift toward a global economy dominated by digital services, innovation, and sectors driven by knowledge. This shift has ignited intense competition among cities and nations vying to become the next tech epicenter, drawing in the top echelons of high-skilled professionals. The educational landscape is swiftly evolving to meet the burgeoning demand for tech talent, marked by the emergence of specialized technical departments and institutions such as Cornell Tech, for-profit coding boot camps such as General Assembly, and an expansive selection of online learning platforms. These entities are dedicated to fostering the development of technological expertise, aligning education with industry needs. In addition, the global mobility of tech professionals is reshaping international dynamics. Advanced economies are refining their immigration policies to attract these highly skilled workers, while emerging economies face the challenge of their brightest minds relocating abroad, leading to a brain drain. Finally, companies are reevaluating their operational models, with a particular emphasis on expanding remote work opportunities as a strategic approach to attract and retain tech talent.[2]

While the term may reverberate as a modern catchphrase in the corridors of corporations and decision makers, for sociologists *tech talent* obscures deeper social problems. Beneath the surface of this label lies a stark reality: persistent disparities along lines of class, gender, race, and age.

The tech industry often venerates a stereotypical image of the "ideal worker"—typically young white men, frequently graduates of elite universities—which permeates hiring practices, workplace culture, and even layoff decisions. This entrenched image highlights a broader narrative of exclusivity and disparity that sidelines women and people of color, despite their abilities and qualifications. In a sector known for high turnover and precarious job security, those who deviate from this conventional mold experience disproportionately high challenges. The chapter delves into the complex demands placed on the so-called ideal worker in the tech industry, which stretch far beyond technical proficiency. These workers are expected to excel in a highly competitive and volatile environment, requiring skills that include rapid adaptation to new technologies, high-level problem solving, and constant innovation. However, the ability to navigate this turbulent landscape is significantly influenced by underlying factors of privilege.

The Dark Side of Tech Talent

The genesis of tech talent can be traced back to the early days of Silicon Valley, during the Cold War, when funding from the U.S. Department of Defense enabled the creation of pivotal technologies, marking the rise of tech specialists as vital national resources. It was here that tech talent first became a national asset; engineers and programmers were recruited to develop cutting-edge technologies for defense and communication networks, such as the Advanced Research Projects Agency Network (ARPANET), which would eventually evolve into the internet we know today. Yet this workforce was significantly composed of white men, a homogeneity that mirrored the exclusionary practices and biases prevalent in mid-twentieth-century America. Notably, the era saw limited participation from women, people of color, and other marginalized groups.[3]

In the 1950s and 1960s, the structure of early tech organizations, including hiring and promotion policies, channeled women into low-status occupations characterized by low wages and limited mobility while racial minorities still remained excluded. Men actively resisted the entry of women into new spheres of technological production, pushing them to work in unskilled jobs for lower salaries. Ironically, one of these low-status professions was software development.[4]

Software development, contrary to its current celebrated high status, was initially seen as a tedious and secretarial profession. Stereotyped as a "social" occupation that required less technical knowledge, it filled a low position in the hierarchy of up-and-coming computer occupations. On the other end, the male-dominated hardware industry was considered pioneering and had high status. This distinction was further fueled by sexist stereotypes about biological differences and cognitive abilities. Women were stereotyped as "naturally" gravitating toward software development because of an "innate" skill set and "analytic mentality" that made them more suitable for that kind of work. As technological and economic advances made software development a more prestigious occupation, women were pushed out of the profession. Tech talent remained a strictly male domain.[5]

The evolution of tech talent also reflects racial disparities, particularly in the early stages of Silicon Valley's development. In the wake of the 1964 Civil Rights Act, U.S. corporations, anticipating new accountability for discriminatory practices, began to slowly diversify their workforces. The Fort Rodman Experiment, initiated by IBM in New Bedford, Massachusetts, is a case in point, representing early efforts to train Black high school dropouts for information technology (IT) roles, driven by the dual goals of fostering government relations and expanding labor pools. Nevertheless, the program's efficacy was hindered by insufficient staffing, inadequate training, and underlying racist paternalistic attitudes inherent to the program's organizers. This led to the program's closure in 1966 amid local community concerns. Diversity initiatives continued at IBM, but nonwhite people were exclusively hired for low-level positions, mirroring broader corporate hiring trends that to this very day relegate Black workers to the lowest wage categories. For example, the average percentage of full-time Black technical employees at IBM today is about the same as it was in 1965: roughly 2.5 percent.[6]

In the late 1960s and early 1970s, thanks to the newly formed venture capital firms such as the Draper and Johnson Investment Company, Silicon Valley became the center of the semiconductor and computer microchip industry. These firms invested heavily in the ideas and start-up companies of young white male technologists who were experimenting with computers and bits of silicon that would become the foundation of the contemporary computer industry. This era saw the rise of hobbyist groups such as the Homebrew Computer Club, where Steve Wozniak and Steve Jobs, cofounders of Apple, among others, exchanged parts, circuits, and the essential knowledge for the construction of early computing devices. As companies such as Intel, Apple, and Hewlett-Packard expanded, there was a growing need for engineers, programmers, and other technically skilled individuals. It was within this milieu that the modern concept of tech talent was born and began to flourish. But as the idea grew, so did the inequality within the field.[7]

The venture capital investors who fueled Silicon Valley's rise and the managers who oversaw the burgeoning ranks of technologists—and who diligently combed through the nation's computer labs and firms for talented workers—were exclusively white men. To these investors, women and racial minorities were largely out of sight. This formative era of venture capital that financed successful start-ups and cultivated a generation of entrepreneurs solidified a culture of gender and racial segregation that continues to impede access for women and racial minorities.[8]

In the 1980s, venture capital investments in Silicon Valley exploded. Software development was no longer seen as inferior to hardware engineering and became recognized as a critical, lucrative sector of corporate America. Employers began hiring computer scientists who had graduated from college with computer science degrees. Yet the new field of software development once again started pushing women out. Hiring women as software developers would not just threaten the newly ascribed prestige of the occupation but would drive down the high salaries that male software developers began to earn.[9]

At the same time, personal computers began flooding the market. As Microsoft and Apple competed to produce the best home computer, millions of households embraced these new machines. The new world of computing, combined with developments in science-fiction cinema and video games, popularized the cultural stereotype of the young white male nerd. "Nerds" and "geeks" had existed since the 1960s and 1970s, solving problems on university-based computers at the Massachusetts Institute of Technology (MIT) and hacking computers using available electronics. Yet the 1980s saw a popularization of this culture especially due to the impact of successful software developers such as Bill Gates, Jobs, and Wozniak, who strengthened the stereotype that the technological geniuses who had become millionaires after launching technology start-ups in their garages were exclusively young white men.[10]

These stereotypes eventually infiltrated the corporate world, leading to the adoption of a "culture fit" requirement for selecting candidates that extended beyond mere aptitude and favored individuals who not only possessed technical skills but also conformed to a specific mold. This preference resulted in the hiring of predominantly "nerdy" unmarried young white men, many deeply engrossed in coding and often voluntarily working late into the night. For managers, these individuals represented the epitome of the ideal worker, as they exhibited intrinsic motivation to foster innovative work practices and contribute to capital accumulation, while their antisocial individualism posed no challenges to managerial authority or the prospect of unionization. The culture associated with computer nerds gave rise to a compelling narrative that prioritized the careers of these ideal workers, ultimately shaping the perception of the ideal worker in the corporate world as synonymous with tech talent.[11]

The emergence of the "nerd" and "geek" cultural stereotypes during the 1980s, popularized through films such as *WarGames* and *Revenge of the Nerds*, alongside the burgeoning video game culture and the association of computers with male domains, profoundly influenced the tech industry beyond mere hiring practices. This cultural shift not only impacted who was hired but also molded the work environments within tech, creating spaces that were often unwelcoming to those who did not fit the emerging stereotype. A masculine ideal that valued technological skill and intellect over physical attributes and athletic prowess fostered a male-dominated culture, hindering women's involvement in software development. In this culture, men compete in technological proficiency and work hours, often to the detriment of women in engineering and computing fields. As a result, nerd and geek masculinity presents a significant barrier for workers in male-dominated workplaces.[12]

From the 1990s to the early 2000s, men largely ousted women from computer professions, dominating roles at all levels. The tech industry favored white and some Asian individuals while marginalizing Black and Latine workers. Despite low national unemployment and significant salary increases in the 1990s, Black and Latine individuals were excluded from high-paying careers. Instead, they found employment in federal government, electronics manufacturing, and lower-tier technical roles. By the early 2000s, software development had become a field predominantly occupied by white and Asian men, many from elite universities, reinforcing a new and powerful cultural stereotype: the "brogrammer."[13]

The brogrammer represents a more recent form of hegemonic masculinity. A combination of *bro* (for *brother*) and *programmer*, *brogrammer* describes a jock-like tech worker whose lifestyle turns workplaces into frat houses. Drinking games, gambling, vulgar pranks, working out, sports activities, and unrestrained male sexual hostility become "labor games" by which brogrammers turn their social and personality traits into desired work practices. These practices are characterized by aggression, competition, and ruthless leadership that see women as sexualized objects to be dominated rather than as competent technical workers on an equal level.[14]

The genesis of this new type of programmer can be traced to Trilogy, a 1990s Silicon Valley start-up that used recruiting strategies to hire recent college graduates with impressive credentials but no work experience from elite private universities. Contrary to the previous generation of introverted and shy nerds and geeks, the brogrammer was exceedingly confident and assertive while also engaging in a "work hard, party harder" lifestyle fueled by openly misogynistic and sexist beliefs.[15]

The influx of software developers who embodied the brogrammer traits increased after the financial crisis of 2008. Business and finance majors who were initially motivated to join Wall Street looked to tech as a way to secure a quick pathway to wealth. Unlike the nerds and geeks of the 1990s, who were entranced by their computer code, brogrammers aimed to solidify their elite socioeconomic status by taking leading roles in up-and-coming start-ups. As fraternity-style games and frat house rites of passage made their way into hiring practices and workplace socialization, women were once again excluded from the networks and opportunities that led to prestigious career tracks.[16]

Brogrammer culture, just like the nerds and geeks phenomenon, also served an important economic function of both recruitment and socialization. It rose to popularity as a means to pull more workers into the high-tech industry. Companies looked beyond the introverted group of nerds and geeks and lured in young, male college students who, in addition to excelling in both math and sports, were business-minded. These workers seemed more on par with the company objectives of aggressive innovation and short-term profits. The demand for brogrammers epitomized employers' demands for a new breed of worker: young white men who were technically talented, assertive, money-driven, and not afraid to take risks.

The tech industry has long faced critical scrutiny for its lack of diversity across gender, race, and age lines. This lack of diversity not only mirrors broader societal inequalities but also raises concerns about the inclusiveness of the technological advancements that shape our world. The culmination of these challenges presents a multifaceted problem: a "tech talent" pool that, until recently, has overlooked the vast potential of women, people of color, and senior individuals.

The Struggle for Diversity

For many years, technology companies did not share information about the diversity of their employees, keeping these details hidden. However, in 2014 the landscape began to shift due to mounting pressures. After facing persistent calls for transparency from the federal government, media, community leaders, and racial justice activists, Yahoo and Facebook started to unveil their employment statistics, categorized by gender and race. Yahoo revealed that Black employees constituted a mere 2 percent of its workforce, while Latine employees made up 4 percent. Similarly, Facebook's workforce data were telling, with only eighty-one Black employees, accounting for a mere 1.5 percent of its 5,500 U.S. workers. These disclosures underscored the glaring racial and gender disparities prevalent within the tech industry, sparking a broader conversation about diversity and inclusion in the sector.[17]

Following the public uproar triggered by the disclosure of their workforce demographics, tech companies attempted to justify the stark underrepresentation of Black and Latine employees. They attributed the disparity to a supposed scarcity of "qualified" Black and

Latine engineers. However, this explanation was quickly challenged by data indicating that prestigious institutions such as Stanford University and MIT were graduating Black and Hispanic students in technical fields at double the rate these leading firms were employing them. This discrepancy exposed the "tech talent shortage" narrative as a mere myth, suggesting that the issue was not a lack of available talent but, rather, the companies' hiring practices and possibly systemic biases within their recruitment processes.[18]

Tech companies were accused not only of prejudicial hiring practices but also of directly discriminating against some of their employees. Workers contended that, on the basis of their race and gender, they were unfairly treated with respect to salary, bonuses, and advancement and accused company managers and colleagues of exposing them to racist and sexist hostility. In 2017, the U.S. Department of Labor sued Oracle for paying white men more than their Black and brown peers with the same job title and for giving preference to immigrant workers, at lower wages, when recruiting to fill technical roles within the company. Facing an expensive legal battle, Oracle agreed to end its discriminatory practices and pay back employees who had been unfairly compensated.[19]

In the same year, numerous women working for Uber, including three Latina software developers, sued the company for allegedly discriminating against women and people of color, claiming they were compensated less because of their gender and race. The lawsuit said Uber used an employee ranking system that was "not based on valid and reliable performance measures" and gave women and Latine, American Indian, and African American employees lower scores than men and white or Asian employees. Uber's senior vice president of engineering and its chief executive at the time, Travis Kalanick, resigned as a result of these lawsuits.[20]

The global walkout staged by more than twenty thousand Google employees on November 1, 2018, marked a significant turning point. Employees took a unified stand against various issues plaguing their workplace, including the company's opacity in decision-making processes, persistent gender and racial disparities, instances of sexual harassment, and contentious collaborations with the military. This protest, though largely symbolic in nature, represented a watershed moment as it demonstrated the tech workforce's growing willingness to openly confront and challenge their employers on matters of ethics, diversity, and workplace culture.[21]

The large-scale protests that followed the murder of George Floyd by a police officer in 2020 forced companies to respond to such criticism. Chief executives and investors who initially limited their support to symbolic tweets eventually promised to invest in initiatives that would promote diversity, equity, and inclusion. Such pledges ranged from donating to Black-owned businesses and changing policies to address hate speech to planning to increase employment and leadership representation of underrepresented groups.

Yet there is little transparency concerning how the total value of $4.56 billion in diversity pledges by tech companies was paid out or to which businesses, founders, or organizations the money went. Evidence suggests that, despite their promises, not a lot has changed. Furthermore, tech companies that made pledges to support racial equality ended up laying off people of color, many of whom worked in so-called support positions in key functions such as diversity and marketing.[22]

High-profile lawsuits and internal investigations at major firms have also shed light on age discrimination. Giants such as Google have been at the center of age discrimination lawsuits regarding unlawful hiring practices. Although it still denies the charges and insists that rejected applicants didn't meet the technical requirements for available jobs, Google was forced to pay compensation to 227 job applicants and set up a committee to address age bias in its hiring practices. Recent class-action lawsuits and investigative reports find that well-established firms such as IBM target senior workers for dismissal during regular reorganizations, seeking to cut "old heads" from the employment rolls. Apart from these lawsuits, though, tech firms have largely escaped scrutiny for ageist termination practices.[23]

The biases present in recruiting algorithms and AI used by companies further complicate the landscape of diversity and inclusion. Automated systems, designed to streamline the hiring process, often replicate and amplify existing biases due to their reliance on historical data. For instance, if an AI recruiting tool is trained on data reflecting a predominantly young, white, and male workforce, it may inadvertently prioritize candidates who fit this profile, excluding or deprioritizing equally qualified candidates from underrepresented groups. This leads to a self-reinforcing cycle in which the existing demographic imbalances are not only maintained but exacerbated by the very technologies that purport to offer unbiased solutions.[24]

The ongoing struggle for diversity in tech underscores the deeply ingrained biases and systemic barriers that continue to pervade the industry. One of these is the persistence of ideal worker norms.

The Ideal Tech Worker

Ideal worker norms are rooted in a gendered division of labor—privileging individuals without caregiving responsibilities—which encompasses tasks such as caring for children, aging parents, and other family members, as well as managing household duties such as cooking and cleaning. Historically, this division has enabled men to dedicate their lives exclusively to paid work, a situation made possible largely because women have assumed the majority of unpaid care work. At the heart of these norms lies the belief that work is a noble endeavor, demanding total commitment and frequent sacrifice from employees.[25]

In the tech industry, the ideal worker stereotype is heavily influenced by an exclusionary culture, often envisioning the ideal worker as a young man. This ideal worker typically holds a computer science degree, possesses the latest technical skills, and can commit to long hours without family or childcare responsibilities. Adding another layer to the already gendered norms of the ideal worker is race. In tech, the archetype often revolves around the young white or Asian man, cultivating a culture that is resistant to addressing racism and discrimination. When confronted, companies typically defend themselves by claiming a meritocratic, color-blind culture, thereby ignoring the significant role of status inequalities in shaping job opportunities.[26]

Yet another facet of the ideal worker transcends demographics, embodying expectations applicable to all workers, though more easily navigated by those in privileged positions. The tech economy, driven by globalization and swift technological advancements, requires a new type of ideal worker. While loyalty is still appreciated, it has evolved from being company-centric to innovation-centric. Consequently, ideal workers now must not only excel in their traditional roles but also adeptly manage the inherent precarity of the industry. This includes being able to navigate rapid change, seize opportunities amid risks, and proactively shape their own career paths in an environment in which job security is increasingly uncertain.[27]

At the apex of the tech industry's hierarchy, where the ideal worker stereotype is sharply defined, a select group of digital elites hold the highest-paying positions within tech firms. These digital elites, typically involved in roles such as software development, possess specialized skills crucial for company growth. Although the tech sector is known for its precarious job security, this privileged class—predominantly young white or Asian men—remains largely insulated from the immediate effects of this instability. Using their networks and prestigious educational backgrounds, they navigate the volatile tech landscape with relative ease, a stark contrast to the experiences of insecurity and instability faced by their less privileged peers. The next chapter delves into the mechanisms that allow these digital elites to thrive amid the instability that affects the broader workforce.[28]

2

Digital Elites

Gregg, thirty-one, a white male software developer, began his career after graduating from a private university in New York City with a degree in computer science. His entry into the field was facilitated by a recommendation from his professor, who had significant connections in New York City's start-up ecosystem. This helped Gregg land a position as a junior software developer, where he found himself among peers—other white men with similar backgrounds and interests—under the leadership of a manager who graduated from the same university. However, a year into his job, the start-up he worked for was acquired by Google, and Gregg suddenly found himself without a job. "It bothered me a little, but I knew that my experiences at this start-up would be advantageous," Gregg said. When Google hired two of his coworkers, Gregg and the manager transitioned to another start-up, a move facilitated by his manager's network.

Gregg's journey through the tech industry unfolded in a pattern that is quite typical within this sector: short tenures at multiple companies. With each move, he gained invaluable experience, expanding his skill set and deepening his comprehension of the software-development life cycle. Despite the tech industry's inherent instability, Gregg saw these changes not as setbacks but, rather, as chances to evolve and adapt. Reflecting on his career shifts, Gregg explained: "Every time I changed jobs, I was confronted with a new set of challenges. Was I anxious? Absolutely. But navigating through those was immensely fulfilling." Now at a logistics start-up, he observes that his journey through various companies has equipped him with a skill set and technological proficiency that stands up to, if not surpasses, that of individuals who have spent years in more traditional, stable positions.

Gregg's maneuvering through the tech industry's volatile landscape isn't merely a reflection of his personal drive. It significantly mirrors his privilege. His choices have been supported by key figures, including his computer science professor, who imparted not only knowledge but also crucial industry connections, and his first manager, who evolved into a mentor, guiding him through career decisions. These relationships have positioned him in an ideal position to game the labor market.

Gaming the Labor Market

Workers such as Gregg exemplify a trend that has become a hallmark of the industry: "job-hopping." Today's tech workers navigate their professional lives through brief stints across various companies, with software developers frequently changing jobs every two years, in stark contrast to the more stable career trajectories of past generations. This practice, while not exclusive to the tech industry, is especially pronounced within it, reflecting a broader shift toward a gig economy mindset. Job-hopping, a strategic response to the industry's rapid innovation and fluctuating project demands, allows workers to amass a diverse skill set, adapt to the evolving technological landscape, and negotiate better positions and salaries.[1]

Job-hopping is heralded as a pathway to career advancement and success. Sheryl Sandberg, former chief operating officer at Facebook/ Meta, once described tech careers as a "jungle gym" rather than a straight ladder, highlighting the value of diverse experiences over linear progression. Rather than indicating inconsistency, changing roles or companies is viewed as ambition and adaptability. For instance, a software developer might gain broader skills and enhance their employability and overall professional growth from four different one-year roles than from five years at a single company.[2]

However, the opportunity to engage in job-hopping is not uniformly accessible to all workers. While mobility is recognized as a key to career progression, only a privileged subset of the workforce can effectively leverage this strategy. This disparity is largely due to the pivotal role of professional networks, which significantly influence the ease with which individuals can transition among roles and companies. Such networks tend to favor a select group of highly esteemed software developers, granting them a unique advantage.[3]

Steven, a thirty-year-old white man, has worked at both Google and Facebook. His career thus far underscores how personal networks play a pivotal role in facilitating movement across prestigious positions. He said:

> Although I have worked with recruiters in the past and have applied to a couple of jobs via traditional job boards and postings and things like that, every job that I have ever taken as a software developer has been because I knew somebody at the company—because I had worked with them, I enjoyed working with them, or they were able to convince me that it was worth my interest.

Successful job-hoppers foster important relationships with key figures in the tech industry either through their jobs or through their educational institutions. This allows them to develop reputations and build valuable professional networks. Ian, a thirty-one-year-old Korean American man who has worked for a series of big tech companies and a start-up in the past five years, explained how important networking has become for software developers. "All my connections came from networking," he said. "At my first job [a start-up] I would regularly go for lunch with my CTO [chief technology officer], sometimes even with the [chief executive]; it helped that the CTO was also Korean American." After the start-up was bought out by Google, Ian and the CTO were hired, a few months apart, at the same big tech company in New York City.

Marius, a thirty-three-year-old white male software developer, provided another illustration of how professional networks can facilitate job transitions in tech. After two years at a start-up, his chief executive, with whom he had built a strong rapport, confidentially informed him about the company's imminent acquisition by a big tech company. Following the acquisition, many software developers, including Marius, were laid off. However, due to the chief executive's assurance and recommendation, Marius quickly secured a position at another start-up. Now employed by a major tech firm after stints at three start-ups in six years, Marius emphasized that a software developer's career is not just about skill sets and hard work. "Successful careers are all about strategizing," he said. "It is about connecting with the right people."

Software developers often engage in job-hopping for a variety of reasons. Topping the list, according to my respondents, is the pursuit of a higher salary. Many of these in-demand professionals, whose technical expertise drives a company's technological achievements, expressed a sentiment of being systematically undercompensated relative to the value they provide. Marc is an artificial intelligence (AI) engineer working at a financial technology (fintech) start-up that provides users with limited funds to buy and sell fractional shares of companies. He is satisfied with his current job, and his salary is a little more than $150,000 a year. He surprised me when he told me that he did not see himself staying at his current company for more than two years: "In tech, you kind of want to move around a lot. It's a red flag if your résumé shows you have been at the same place for six years." When I asked whether there was something about his current company that made him want to leave, he complained that he was not adequately compensated. "After sticking around at the same company for three years, you level up from an intermediate to an advanced programmer," he said. "During that time, you might get a 20 percent raise, but honestly, you're bringing like 40–50 percent more value to the table. To really cash in on that added value, you've got to jump ship to another company." George, a twenty-eight-year-old white male software developer, transitioned from a digital fitness start-up to Amazon and pointed out the financial benefits of such a move. He mentioned that, when switching companies, one can see an average pay boost of about 7–10 percent. "This rate is much higher than the yearly raise I'd get if I stayed put at my current company," he remarked.

Job-hopping extends beyond the mere pursuit of higher salaries. Numerous developers have cited feelings of stagnation when tethered to one company for extended periods. This sense of inertia often arises from limited growth opportunities within the organization, combined with an environment that might feel uninspired and a strong desire to familiarize oneself with new technological frameworks. James, a twenty-seven-year-old white male software developer working at a small tech firm that provides software to financial entities, underscored this sentiment. Having previously been part of Google, he advocated that changing roles can be instrumental in updating one's skill set. This perspective led him back to the start-up environment, where he initially began his professional journey:

> I have moved around a lot, and not just because I want more money. To get ahead in tech, which literally changes every month, you really need to know your stuff. Having superficial knowledge will hurt you in the long run. So moving companies is a way to keep learning. This might be unfortunate for companies because they are hiring someone who might be gone soon. For me personally, it is not something I want to keep doing for the rest of my life.

Despite earning a salary of approximately $250,000 a year, James felt dubious about changing jobs so often; he had changed jobs six times in the previous five years. He felt that he might be overdoing it and might perhaps be in danger of being stigmatized as a "disloyal employee." But even when he felt at home at some companies he worked for, interacted well with colleagues and management, worked on interesting projects, and saw potential in his role, he decided to seek employment elsewhere. James felt that by "getting too comfortable," he would be sidetracked from the real task at hand: to have transferable skills, a rich résumé, and a vast arsenal of technological tools. Staying at a company for more than five years would put him at a huge disadvantage:

If I stay here for too long, I will not have many options in the future. My growth might be significant within the company, and I might be rocking their stack for years to come. But I will not be growing alongside the market. My skills and connections won't matter in five years' time when I apply for another job.

Job-hopping also enables software developers to bypass traditional career-progression structures, granting them higher status without necessarily navigating through established hierarchies. Ishaan, a thirty-three-year-old Asian American man, pointed out that this approach is particularly feasible in young, emerging companies that may not have rigorous hiring protocols: Start-ups sometimes miss implementing effective assessment techniques, which can allow software developers to secure positions that might exceed their skill levels. "If someone can persuade the management about their expertise or their vision for a product, it doesn't necessarily mean they're the optimal choice for the role or that their designated title genuinely mirrors their true competence," Ishaan said. This is known as job title inflation—the practice of giving employees titles that may not accurately reflect their actual roles, responsibilities, or experience levels. This phenomenon tends to be more prevalent in start-ups, which generally have standardized job titles consistent across the industry. James, a thirty-seven-year-old white man, is now a vice president of engineering. He humorously remarked that he held the same job title thirteen years earlier at an early-stage New York City start-up as he does now, working at a big tech company:

> I graduated from Stanford with a computer science degree and became a lead engineer at a small start-up that eventually got bought out by Google. I thought I had reached my apex at twenty-two. [Laughs] Little did I know . . . that I didn't know anything! Maybe they wanted me to stay, so they gave me everything a kid straight out of college would want.

For Jason, a software developer, job title inflation worked in his favor. He admitted that becoming a lead engineer in a team of three people without any prior supervisory experience was out of the ordinary, but he used the situation to his advantage. His next company, also a start-up, offered him a better salary and a position with increased responsibilities. His short stint at a start-up that was acquired by Google helped him stand out from other potential candidates. His move after a year and a half exposed him to a range of technologies and business solutions that he would not have the chance to learn if he had stayed at the same company for more than five years.

Job title inflation, although beneficial at the start of one's career, can stifle professional growth in the future. Amassing inflated job titles on one's résumé can lead to expedited vertical career growth, when a worker attains a flashy job title and high salary without having climbed the standard steps of the career ladder. As a result, when this worker moves from one job to another, they may miss horizontal career growth, gaining the skills, experience, and knowledge required to keep moving up. For Jin, a thirty-five-year-old Asian American man, job-hopping meant gaining short-term prestige and salary hikes, but it also caused him to struggle at a later stage in his career:

> I thought I would get better money if I jumped around. For a time, I certainly did. At times I felt like a giant imposter, to be honest. I didn't really have something to show. I could do the job but could not stand out. I'm staying put now to develop something I can later sell.

The experiences of software developers described so far underscore a broader imperative: the relentless pursuit of adaptability and continuous learning. In an industry characterized by rapid technological advancements and evolving project demands, the ability to swiftly adapt and master new technologies is not just an advantage—it's a necessity. This environment has given rise to a culture where staying static is synonymous with falling behind. Software developers find themselves in a perpetual cycle of learning, not only to enhance their immediate job performance, but also to secure their relevance in the future job market. Thus, a powerful ethos emerges that drives professionals to remain on the cutting edge of technological progress.

This constant state of flux challenges software developers to redefine what it means to be successful, emphasizing flexibility, lifelong learning, and the strategic navigation of career opportunities as key components of professional growth.

Adapt or You Will Be Replaced

> A real engineer will adapt. I have strategically changed my roles at different companies since the beginning of my career. You can consider it entrepreneurial. I follow what is best for me, for my value as an expert. I started as an electrical engineer, then I was working as site support or what they call DevOps, then mobile engineer, after this as a full-stack engineer. Right now, I am an AI engineer. I chose these roles very carefully and very strategically.
> —Rashid

Rashid, a thirty-year-old Asian male software developer, epitomizes the characteristics of a digital elite by offering a perspective that's emblematic of the tech industry. "Adapt or you will be replaced" is an established truth among software developers. For Rashid it embodies an adaptive spirit that has seen him change his skill sets according to the industry's demands. What we see here as job-hopping also allows software developers to continuously upskill and select specific job titles, capturing the attention of recruiters and hiring managers.

Take, for instance, the designation "full-stack developer." Such professionals possess expertise in both the back-end and front-end facets of applications, websites, or programs. They are proficient in drafting the intricate computer code required for system functionality (the back end) and simultaneously possess the flair for designing aesthetic and intuitive user interfaces (the front end). Adopting the "full-stack" title can be a strategic move for software professionals. By showcasing their versatility across various phases of software development, they often command more job opportunities and higher salaries.[4]

Typically, full-stack developers were hired only at start-ups. Running a start-up that is more than likely "bootstrapped"—that is, relying on savings and revenue to operate rather than venture capital or outside investment—means that fewer employees are needed to complete more tasks. Full-stack developers become much-needed generalists who can commit to all stages of the product development and be flexible about working with new technologies. Although still early in his career, Bryan, a twenty-eight-year-old Asian American man who was interviewing for start-up jobs at the time of our interview, boosted his chances of being hired by claiming to be a full-stack generalist. "Nowadays, you got to know a little bit of everything," he said "When I interview for start-ups, they tell me everyone needs to do a little bit of everything. So your best shot is to say that you are a full-stack engineer. You want to give yourself the best chance."

Branding oneself as full stack, in addition to making claims to a generalist professional status, conveys an approach to work that employers find very attractive. Jeremy, a thirty-eight-year-old white man who works as a software development manager at a start-up, said that full-stack developers should embody "determination and tenacity" and were willing to "engage in continuous learning that will cover a wide breadth of technologies." Moreover, full-stack developers should ideally be "coding mavericks"—that is, not afraid to go about their work autonomously, without having to coordinate with other employees. Jeremy said:

> Every company nowadays wants to hire full-stack developers. They are the best problem solvers, in my opinion. A good full stack will have a broad set of technical skills to help your business expand. But more importantly, they can do the work that two to three people would do, which is great for cost-efficiency.

Full-stack developers are beneficial to the employer because they promise a cheaper source of labor. Start-ups and small firms can hire a generalist full-stack developer if they cannot afford an entire team of specialists. Moreover, generalists, according to Jeremy, bypass the counterproductive "bureaucratic inertia" typical to larger companies that prevent the efficient operation of a company's core activities. Full-stack developers' ability to work on any part of the product typically makes them ideal candidates for companies that want to save costs and, at the same time, ensure fast product innovation and development.

Although many software developers I interviewed were very eager to describe themselves to me as "full stack," others were skeptical about the title. According to Leo, a thirty-seven-year-old white male software developer, it is simply impossible to be a true full stack:

> If you are working at a start-up with five people, I can see why being a generalist would suit your company's needs better. But if you want to work here, you need expert-level knowledge. New grad engineers might call themselves "full stack," but they have no concept of what the inner workings of an HTTP [hypertext transfer protocol] request is because they're used to working in a higher level of abstraction that hides those details. They might know [the JavaScript library] React but be totally ignorant of fundamental considerations.

Yet for full-stack developers such as Aziz, a software developer from India in his early thirties who began his career specializing in front-end development but transitioned to full-stack development to stay competitive, calling oneself a full-stack developer is not just a way to market oneself as a software development generalist. It is necessary to meet the demands of the industry. Not being a full-stack developer means that one might fall behind in one's career:

> Front-end development has been expanding. You have new libraries and frameworks, like React. These have introduced back-end concepts to the language. Gone are the days where you would just have a traditional front-end role that would ignore the back end. Gone are the days where you would have a back-end role that didn't do anything on the front end. You also need to know how to set up servers, despite AWS [the Amazon Web Services platform] telling you to go serverless. You should also know how to test code, quality assurance. You either do it all or nothing.

Aziz, like many software professionals I interviewed, realizes that full-stack development, just like other new job titles, means that workers in the coming years must be open to learning a broader range of technical skills. This means that developers and engineers must increasingly frame their work as generalists and understand multiple technological stacks if they are going to build better applications and therefore be more employable.

Another job title that software developers adopt for personal branding is "data scientist." Data scientists are lionized as much needed talent who provide the ability to "extract, refine and deploy this new source of value in the global economy."[5] These emerging roles are presented as "must skills" for information technology (IT) workers who will foster further innovation across fields such as AI. Data scientists become culturally significant for aspiring software developers. The *Harvard Business Review* went as far as to call data science "the sexiest job of the 21st century," and several universities have launched data science programs, such as New York University's Center for Data Science and Columbia University's Data Analytics Bootcamp.[6]

Building a personal brand that conveys technical expertise as a data scientist becomes an essential strategy for software developers. As companies not just in tech but in the finance, health-care, media and entertainment, and logistics industries try to capitalize on the advent of data science technologies, demand is rising for software developers who can deliver such applications. But a data scientist should not only show competence in technical skills. "You need to bridge the gap between technology and business," a 2018 LinkedIn article explains; software developers must be able to translate their projects into products, services, or improved business processes.[7]

Software developers must add an extra layer to their personal branding strategy: They must also have a feel for business issues and empathy for customers. When I asked interviewees how they felt about such an adaptation to the world of business, some saw it as an opportunity to become a "jack of all trades." One of those people was Cho, a thirty-six-year-old Asian American man who started as a software developer and now leads a team at a medium-size company that specializes in media curation. "If you really want to shine as a data scientist, you need to convince people you are a magician," Cho told me. "It's all about the personality and attitude." Such "magicians" do not necessarily have to be the world's best technical coders, but they need to share the company's vision for the product in the making. They need to demonstrate a passionate desire to contribute to the success of the company.

Coding Alone

> We all have this desire to learn, to build, and to solve problems. If we feel we are in a job that is not fulfilling our curiosity, we will move on to another company. When I changed jobs, I was tasked with distilling and refining a new set of problems. This was an attractive and very rewarding process. I gained a fundamental understanding of logistics that I initially didn't know anything about. Now, after a few years, I probably know more than people who have worked in more traditional companies within logistics their entire careers.
>
> —Jeremy

Workers such as Jeremy, the thirty-eight-year-old software developer, epitomize the digital elite's career mindset: Work is passion. On the surface, this looks like a win-win situation. Workers have the opportunity to engage with building technologies, an area they are passionate about, while employers benefit from having employees who are fully committed to the company's vision. However, the work-as-passion approach places the entire burden of career progression on individual workers. Innovative ideas and personal projects, born from genuine creativity, become strategic investments to secure future employment opportunities. At the same time, any collective effort to improve working conditions is perceived as a hindrance to one's career. The digital elites embody a "me against the world" mentality.[8]

Lawrence, who has spent more than a decade in Silicon Valley, has become increasingly critical of tech's individualist culture. The pursuit of new ideas, while driving technological progress, often comes at a cost. "Techies are obsessed with tackling problems independently," Lawrence remarked, "but it's a fine line before this morphs into a culture rife with self-absorption and narcissism." The ideal tech worker is often depicted as a maverick—a genius who innovates without the need for support. This myth not only glorifies the "lone wolf" archetype. It also discourages the community-oriented ethos that could support more collaboration both in the workplace and as an organizing effort.[9]

The emphasis on individualism overlooks the tight-knit networks that enable certain individuals to thrive. This ties into the notion of meritocracy. When successful people discuss how they achieved their status, many cite hard work and perseverance, often overlooking other factors that contributed to their success. Furthermore, the emphasis on individualism and meritocracy attributes failures solely to the individual and thus promotes a work environment that overlooks structural inequalities. On the contrary, the individualist approach exacerbates inequality by isolating failures as personal shortcomings rather than systemic problems. When digital elites fail, they often blame themselves.[10]

The software developers discussed in this chapter are comfortable with the industry's instability, largely due to their privileged position. However, the workers described in the next three chapters do not share this privilege or comfort. Although the tech industry encourages workers to be motivated by passion, it also establishes significant barriers for women, people of color, and senior workers. These workers must navigate an unstable labor market and take risks while simultaneously experiencing marginalization and exclusion from networks, mentorships, and career opportunities. This makes it exceedingly challenging for them to find opportunities in precarious work.

3

Pretty Colors and Cleaning Up

Dawn, a thirty-year-old software developer, has often found herself as one of the few women in her field. From being one of only two women in her college graduating class to her seven years in the tech industry, she has experienced firsthand the unwelcoming environment for women in technology. In 2018, Dawn joined a large number of tech workers who organized protests to demand better working conditions. This collective action marked a pivotal moment in advocating for change within the industry. The subsequent years, particularly after the mass mobilizations in in 2020, saw tech companies publicly committing to diversity initiatives. However, for Dawn and many like her, these measures have yet to address the root of the problem fully.

While there has been some increase in the number of women in certain sectors, significant barriers still hinder their participation and advancement, particularly in technical roles such as software development. Dawn observed that, even with diversity initiatives aimed at increasing the number of women in tech, a troubling trend remains: Many women hired as software developers find themselves funneled into less technical roles. For example, a colleague of Dawn's, Hannah, was initially hired as a junior software developer but soon found herself nudged toward front-end development, a field focused more on the aesthetic and user-interface aspects of software. This shift, seemingly based on the assumption that her interpersonal and artistic skills would better serve this area, underscores a persistent bias in company culture. Such biases subtly steer women away from the technical trajectories they aspire to follow.

This chapter shows how women continue to encounter an exclusionary tech culture that pressures them to pivot to roles perceived as more aligned with societal expectations of their gender. It is these roles that also exhibit more precarity, temporary work, and wage inequity. The issue of gender inequality is therefore compounded by the precarious nature of certain tech jobs, which tend to channel workers into feminized, less secure sub-occupations such as front-end development and software testing. These roles, which focus on aesthetics and user interaction, are frequently filled through short-term contracts. Although the positions may offer higher salaries compared with those of traditionally precarious jobs, they come with their own set of challenges: unpredictability, excessive workloads, high turnover rates, and scant benefits. For women in tech, these difficulties are intensified by the widespread discrimination they face, adding an extra layer of hardship to their professional lives. Thus, while software jobs are often perceived as stable and meritocratic, the reality reveals a gendered precarization of even high-status technical roles. One of these is front-end web development.[1]

Pretty Colors

Joy is a twenty-seven-year-old white woman who graduated from a private university in New York City in 2014 with a degree in computer science. She described her experience at her first two jobs as "disappointing." When she was a junior software developer, her managers at the two start-ups she worked for repeatedly told her that her skill set was too limited. "I would go home and continue coding, just to prove to everyone that I had what it takes," Joy explained. "I had no mentor at work, so I relied on online communities and friends to share their insights with me." At her first job, Joy was pushed into the more feminized field of front-end software development. "My manager, who did not have a technical background, told me I had an 'eye for design' and that I was 'good with graphics,' even though I had a degree in computer science," Joy explained. "Women hear this all the time: 'You are good with colors,' which is a nice way of saying, 'We do not want you to work on the technical stuff.'"

After two years, Joy was hired at a similar-size start-up as a full-stack developer. She was going to be responsible for both the front end (client side) and back end (server side) of the company's product. Yet it turned out that her new role was predominantly front end. She was again asked to work on design rather than the inner workings of software. Her male colleagues were handpicked by management to work with algorithms. "On the back end you had dudes that were praised for their approach to problem solving; on the front end, they praised my intuition and artistic approach, even though I had studied algorithms in college," Joy said. To make matters worse, she was paid less than her male colleagues.

While being pushed further into the field she was trying to move out of, Joy realized that front-end development was also much less secure than working with the back-end side of software. The projects she worked on were being dictated by shifting client demands, which meant erratically changing requirements and longer working hours. At the same time, the front-end landscape was always in flux due to new technologies being introduced every few months. This caused Joy to constantly play catch-up with new technologies and invest extra time in learning and predicting where the market would go. She had heard horror stories from friends working for companies that outsourced their front-end projects to cut costs and laid off front-end developers, giving more proof of their low status and dispensability. Moreover, Joy was under enormous pressure to work extra hard so her coworkers and manager would not judge her performance on the basis of her gender. But after almost two years at the company, she gave her two weeks' notice and started applying for other jobs.

Near the end of 2018, Joy was hired by one of the FAANG (Facebook, Apple, Amazon, Netflix, Google) companies. At first, she felt that her luck had changed. Her annual salary was slightly higher, an improvement from her previous two jobs, but still less than $100,000.

Joy was hired to work on a team that developed digital tools using map data. "It was exciting even though I was the only woman in a team of ten workers," she told me. As time went by, she became ostracized by the group of insular and introverted male peers. She frequently found herself the recipient of sexist jokes and comments, in addition to being doubted as a technologist. "I was never accepted as one of them," she said. "We did not communicate, and they refused to include me, [and] when they did, I was that front-end chick who didn't know anything."

At the end of the second quarter, during personnel review, management characterized her as an "excellent team player" but working in the wrong department and steered her to apply to other positions in the firm not directly related to software development. "I was taken out of the team and placed in the product design department of the company," Joy said. "I found myself working with mostly women for the first time; that is when I finally came to terms with what was really going on."

Joy continued to work on the front end, still stuck in a field far from the type of work for which her degree had prepared her—and what she wanted to work on. Although she had planned to keep searching for a job in software development, the uncertainty of the job market once the COVID-19 pandemic began forced her to remain at her current job. "I was lucky that I did not lose my job," she told me during a follow-up interview, "but I am still planning to escape the front end."

The demoted position of front-end developers in the gendered division of labor exposes women to precarious work characterized by short-term and fast-changing job requirements. Competition among companies and aggressive innovation require workers to keep up with a continuously growing client base. As users expect more from both online and mobile applications, front-end developers are responsible for always creating the best user experience. To cut costs, companies convert front-end work from full-time to project-based jobs, with front-end developers working as independent contractors, hired only to design and create the interface of an application; they are let go once the project is over. Ann, a white front-end developer in her late twenties, explained that this is a corporate strategy that benefits men:

> It does not make sense for companies to invest in front-end developers when they don't know what the stack will be in a few months' time. You hire a [front-end] developer because you need them now. It does not make sense to keep and train them. Those that are trained and fast-tracked into management, it's mostly guys on the back end. So you learn how to work fast, change stacks, and get comfortable with little or no supervision.

The project-based nature of front-end development and the barring of women from advanced career tracks cause workers to lose access to valuable training and mentorship programs that will help them advance their careers. "How can I move forward when I'm stuck in the front end?" Portia, a twenty-eight-year-old white female programmer working in front-end development asked. "To manage a team, I need to know both back end and front end, and I need mentorship."

Yet without access to anything but the job she is expected to do as a front-end developer, career advancement becomes extremely difficult, which also results in lower and stagnant salaries. Female front-end software developers therefore experience a glass ceiling both because of their gender and because of the type of technology into which they are pushed. By contrast, working in front-end development frequently becomes a stepping stone for men to more prestigious career tracks. "The sky is the limit for them," Portia told me. "We [women] are pushed to work with product design, and guys are encouraged to move into machine learning, big data, etcetera."

Excluded from mentorship and training programs, female front-end developers must continuously rely on their own initiative and self-directed learning to progress as software developers. This involves working on side projects and studying during one's free time, even after work. "Front-end development forces you to become self-taught," Portia explained. However, remaining knowledgeable about a range of frameworks becomes an arduous task in a constantly changing technological landscape. "If you decide to lose focus for a few months, you will have a huge handicap."

Adding to this challenge is the extremely fragmented world of front end, a topic that came up repeatedly during interviews. Some described learning front end as navigating a maze that involves a lot of guessing about what frameworks companies will end up using. Contrary to the back end, which is more established across company settings, the front end was described as "unending," adding to the problems already being experienced by workers.

In the past few years, front-end development has experienced immense growth as companies prioritize how software applications will appeal to established and new clients. Companies such as Facebook, whose business models revolve around advanced user experiences, develop new frameworks such as React, radically altering the area of front-end development. Changes in serverless computing pioneered by Amazon Web Services (AWS) demonstrate how even prestigious software roles can become precarious due to automation. As a result of these recent changes, a *new* gendered divide has occurred *within* the growing field of front-end development, which transfers the burden of precarious work to those working on the more creative part of building an application.

"You now have two types of front-end developers," Ann explained. "Guys are encouraged to do more JavaScript-focused programming, and then you have developers who focus on HTML and CSS [Cascading Style Sheets], the User Interface [UI], and User Experience [UX]." Front-end developers are pushed to do design and artistic work rather than build software. "The guys that work on JavaScript stuff become front-end 'engineers' or 'architects,'" Ann added, "and women become front-end 'designers' or 'visualizers.'"

Despite having technical backgrounds in computer science, female software developers find themselves in a devalued position and exposed to more insecure work conditions. "Most [front-end design] work is at the start of a product, which means designers are more likely to be hired for a project, not full time," Ann explained. Such contracts are either short-term, ranging from a few weeks to a few months, or fixed-term, contracts that are a year long with contingencies attached for renewal. Such contract work provides no added benefits, including sick leave, other health benefits, and opportunities for skills training or conference expenses.[2]

In the world of design, contract work is often celebrated as giving workers more autonomy, flexibility, and higher status because these jobs are "cool" and found in "hot" industries. We see a similar dynamic for front-end designers working for tech companies. At the same time, front-end designers are pressured by management to embrace such careers because they are more suited to doing creative work. Denied the opportunity to develop their technical expertise, women are encouraged to apply for short-term positions that require "compassionate" and "client-centered" workers who can create "beautiful" products. Although contract work is often seen as a choice and a form of empowerment for the worker, what we see is that a segment of the tech labor force is pushed to these nonstandard work arrangements within the context of a gendered division of labor.[3]

Cleaning Up

Software testing is another sub-occupation within software development that is described as gendered and characterized by precarious working conditions—namely, high turnover and poor career advancement opportunities. In the United States, where two-thirds of all testers are found in high-tech industries, 31–35 percent of software testers are women. Software testing can be described as the underlying glue that holds together the compiled source code of tech companies' software applications. Simply put, software testing verifies that a software application's functions operate in conformance with their behavioral requirement specifications, ensuring structural integrity and quality.[4]

Although software testing is a vital part of software development, it is often seen as less creative than "pure" software development. Maxine, a thirty-eight-year-old white senior software test engineer, explained that although testers' work is often ignored, they make up a vital part of the software development process.[5] "When you think of a software developer, who do you picture?" she asked. "Someone writing brilliant code, right? Wrong! A common misconception is that we just build stuff, but for the ones in the trenches, it's all about repair. . . . Yes, it's all about the bugs!"

In the companies Maxine worked for, most of her colleagues in the developer and engineering roles were men. While working in testing, she encountered more female colleagues. Now, as a senior engineer, she explains that testers are not always taken seriously in the world of software development: "Throughout my career, I always had developers telling me my job was easy and that they could write automated tests in a few days. . . . But I was the one cleaning their mess at the end of the day by identifying bugs in their code."

Stereotypes frequently make their way into descriptions of such professional distinctions. Michael, a forty-year-old white software development manager, highlighted some stereotypes when he described the types of workers who gravitate toward software testing: "People who innovate and are competitive are more likely to engage in programming. Testers care more about the user. Software testing values certain attributes, like communication skills, patience, and responsiveness." When I read this quote to Maxine, she laughed and replied, "I am not sure how I would react if I were younger." During her early career, when she participated in meetings with the developer team, her technical expertise was frequently doubted due to her gender. "I was talked over in meetings and frequently dismissed," she said. "I developed a thick skin because of that." Her male colleagues would frequently use aggression to win arguments, even when a point of dispute was within her domain. "They could not accept the fact they were being proven wrong by a tester *and* a woman," she said. The great thing about being a tester, however, according to Maxine, is that despite the gendered attributes they are ascribed, testers always have the final word: "At the end of the day, even though we are often questioned and doubted, we control the quality of the final product, not them."

The work of testers, in addition to being lower paid and less prestigious, is more often characterized by short-term work and project-based contracts. Especially early on in their careers, many testers find it very difficult to secure permanent work. "I think most of us land a permanent job after the first five years," Heather, a thirty-three-year-old white software tester, explained. "Others are not so lucky and just move around a lot." The bulk of open tester jobs, especially at large, established companies, tend to be contract positions with the possibility of being hired as a permanent employee at the end of the contract. Contracts can be offered for anywhere from three months to one-and-a-half years. "When I worked at a major tech company as a tester, my contract lasted for almost one-and-a-half years," Heather noted. "But after I was released, I couldn't work there again for a whole year."

Heather ended up working in a series of contract positions, which caused tech companies not to hire her as a full-time employee because they questioned her loyalty. Moreover, it was not uncommon that contracts ended early, without any warning. "Many contracted positions have no fixed end date, with multiple extensions," she explains. "This made me feel not just disrespected but very anxious about the future."

Contract workers in technology industries must frequently show proactive commitment to stand out to management. Such dedicated willingness to do the job, despite an insecure future, is a hallmark of both the new economy and the tech industry. Yet for women who are sex-typed in undervalued positions such as testing, engaging in such emotional labor must take place in a hostile gendered work environment. "How can you be confident when they don't take you seriously?" Heather asked. "How can you show your value when they do not value you as an employee?"

Although the tech industry prides itself on being a meritocracy, women are expected to be docile and agreeable, traits that limit their productivity. Confidence is reserved for male developers, who are more often seen as showing the behavior of "natural" leaders. When female colleagues are devalued both as women and as testers, they often find it exceedingly difficult to show proactive commitment and dedication and to stand out in the workplace. "Companies treat testers like janitors, not like technical professionals," Mia, a twenty-eight-year-old Asian American software developer, explained. Mia started as a tester but eventually transferred to DevOps, which involves the integration of development and IT operations to streamline software delivery and infrastructure management. She further explains how the negative view toward testers overlaps with how managers treat women:

> When I worked as a tester, most of my colleagues were women. We had to work on a different floor than the dudes in the development team. Although we were working on the same project, we only met during monthly meetings. Those were mostly unilateral, telling us to "hurry up and finish debugging." After a year, I had no intention of remaining at such a place.

Testing, like other software occupations, is characterized by a high turnover rate. Testers are often seen as expendable workers who are useful for only one phase of software development, typically coming in for a specific task and leaving once it is completed. "They see us like the cleaning crew," Mia said. "We are hired near the end of the project, and once we are done, we are out the door." Managers ignore the fact that testing is a meticulous process that requires time. "Job burnout is very prevalent among testers. We don't get paid enough, our work is rushed, and *we* are responsible for any mistakes," Mia told me. "A lot of people can't handle that."[6]

Testers are considered low status and occupy a lower position in the software hierarchy than software developers. Despite this, some of the male software developers I interviewed explained that they had worked as testers early in their careers before transferring to other departments. Such a strategic career move is harder for women. "There is an assumption that if you ever worked as a tester, you do not know how to code; that you are not technical," Mia explained. "However, I have seen male testers receive far more support in their choices to gain more developer skills. It seems that *their* passion is more important than our passion."

Sandra, a twenty-nine-year-old white software developer, is an exception in this phenomenon. She worked as a tester for six years and is now a senior software developer at a software company in New York City. She managed to gain experience and eventually move into a development role by working for multiple start-ups early in her career. When she started her career at a large company, she observed that some junior workers "walked in as testers and left as software developers" after a year. "Management mentored these guys so they could start writing automation tests rather than manually test for bugs, something that I had to do," Sandra explained. "They became what they call 'Software Development Engineer in Test' [SDET] and advertised themselves as developers rather than testers." Realizing that she would not be able to escape her role as a tester, Sandra worked for a string of start-ups before being hired full time by her current company. At start-ups, the line between testers and developers was blurrier than in the larger organization for which she had worked. Working as a tester at start-ups with fewer employees allowed her to work closely with software developers. "After four years, I gained valuable experience working side by side with the developers instead of just focusing on my role," she said.

Sandra's case is an example of how female software developers must engage in even more job-hopping than men. Furthermore, the privileged position of men allows them to change companies out of choice rather than necessity. Women's searches for new jobs are fueled by general disappointment with corporate culture and a disillusionment with companies' diversity initiatives. Increasing numbers of scandals, not just about sexual harassment but also about privacy and facilitation of extremist ideologies, create a stark mismatch between what engineers and developers believe in and what tech companies' priorities are. "I feel many of my colleagues, especially women, job-hop out of necessity; as long companies refuse to address employee needs, we will look for something better," Dawn told me.[7]

Beyond Diversity Initiatives

Since the early 2010s, the percentage of women in computer science undergraduate programs has modestly increased, recovering from a significant decline in the mid-1980s. This gradual improvement is largely attributed to numerous initiatives aimed at encouraging women to pursue careers in tech, which have contributed to narrowing the gender gap in science, technology, engineering, and mathematics (STEM) education. "Computer science today is attracting a more creative type of worker, which specifically targets women," notes Linda Sax, an education professor at the University of California, Los Angeles. "Tech companies are realizing that innovation can no longer continue unless they first solve the problem of diversity."[8] The writing of computer code, the backbone of software building, is now being portrayed as something different. No longer an esoteric craft belonging to the insular world of male nerds, or a business-centered, cut-throat profession dominated by brogrammers, coding is being represented as more social and friendly to women.[9]

Although getting more women into computing is a well-intentioned policy, it will have little effect if existing organizational practices and hierarchies remain in place. Increasing the number of women in the tech pipeline may cause employment levels to rise, but women may continue to be relegated to insecure tech roles. At the same time, prestigious jobs may remain exclusively in the hands of male workers who continue to occupy leadership positions in both technical and nontechnical departments at successful tech companies. It awaits to be seen whether addressing the exclusionary organizational environments prevalent in tech companies will address the structural problems that generate a gendered division of labor and precarious work conditions.

Gender discrimination cases in the technology industry often concern not only gender but also race. Women of color are affected especially by gender discrimination as they face two vectors of oppression: sexism and racism. The cumulative effect of such discrimination is compounded by a striking lack of racial diversity at tech companies. Historically, people of color have long been excluded from the tech industry, along with being relegated to jobs in the secondary labor market. Central to such exclusion is a racialized framing of intelligence, labor fitness, and technical skill by dominant racial groups. In the next chapter, I explore this process by focusing on workers' exposure to both racialized and gendered conceptions of labor fitness and precarious work conditions in the tech industry.

4

"Excuse Me! Do You Work Here?"

I work as a software developer for a big tech company, and they organized an event to promote a new tool that my team and I built. I was going to that place, and I was running a little late. There was a lady that was hosting the event and signing people in, and as I approached her, she looks at me, eyes wide open, with awe and shock. She is Black, too, and she points to her skin and says, "You are the first one!" Then I walk in. It is a huge crowd, and I'm the only Black person there. People stare at me as if I just walked into the wrong place. "Can I help you?" someone asks me. . . . How can you not let this take over your mind?
—Anthony

At Google, Anthony, a thirty-two-year-old software developer, feels like an outsider among his colleagues: Black employees constitute less than 2 percent of the technical staff. "It's just two of us on my floor," Anthony said. But before even reaching his floor, another layer of differentiation becomes apparent: the red sticker on his badge that has to be validated by security. This marker indicates his status as a temporary worker within the company. Anthony is also part of Google's shadow workforce, composed of temps and contractors, which outnumbers the company's full-time employees. Though Anthony often works alongside full-time employees, he was hired through an external recruiter and earns less than the employees, receives fewer benefits, and lacks paid vacation time. This two-tier employment system has significant implications for workers such as Anthony. Being Black and a temporary worker exacerbates the sense of exclusion and isolation he faces every day.[1]

Anthony's career has been marked by significant challenges from the outset. During his college years in computer science, he felt out of place, surrounded predominantly by white peers. He often experienced microaggressions, with some classmates even questioning his presence in the program. This unsettling experience extended into his professional life at Google, where he was subjected to routine badge checks by colleagues, underscoring his perceived outsider status. Despite being highly visible as one of the only two Black employees on his floor, Anthony frequently experienced a sense of invisibility, often overlooked by mentors and feeling undervalued in a workplace that seemed indifferent to his contributions and presence.

Anthony's experience mirrors that of many Black tech workers. As this chapter shows, a common thread is profound exclusion from the sector. This exclusion manifests in two ways: first, on an employment basis, and second, in isolation. Nonwhite tech workers, already severely underrepresented, face barriers in hiring; limited career opportunities, such as mentorship and networking; and, therefore, restricted career progression. Such disparities further entrench the precarious working conditions in tech, pushing especially workers of color into lower-status job roles marked by instability, reduced wages, and excessive workload demands. Yet exclusion also describes the profound isolation Black workers experience navigating the white spaces of tech workplaces. My respondents explained that, regardless of the job-related challenges, the constant feeling of being outsiders was the most exhausting. It comes as no surprise that Black and Latine software workers exit the tech industry at the highest rates.[2]

Getting In

Olivia, a twenty-four-year-old Black woman, graduated from her local Brooklyn college with a degree in computer science and a minor in mathematics. Her passion for numbers and algebra earned her a scholarship and steered her toward software development. However, entering the job market proved challenging. Despite references from her college professors, she struggled to land a job interview; she faced a series of rejections, and many companies did not even bother to respond. Mounting frustration led her to accept a temporary position as a network support specialist at Amazon, which, disappointingly, did not allow her to work on software development. Over the next two years, she finally secured a software development role at a financial institution. Though elated, she reflected on the exhausting process of breaking through the hiring phase. "If I had studied at a more prestigious university, I would have been hired more easily, even though I am just as good," she said, her voice tinged with frustration.

Early in her career, Olivia noted the critical role of networks and connections within the industry, which seemed to fast-track the hiring process for more privileged individuals. Reflecting on her experiences, she commented: "It felt like no matter how hard I worked or what I achieved, I was invisible to those with the power to hire." Her fate ended up in the hands of recruiters, who, acting as the industry's gatekeepers, typically draw from applicant pools that reflect their existing social networks, which are often composed of individuals from similar racial, educational, and professional backgrounds. For example, recruiters might show bias toward candidates who have interned at well-known tech companies, overlooking the potential of candidates with experience at smaller firms or those who have developed portfolios through self-directed projects or community-driven initiatives.[3]

As Olivia navigated the hiring landscape, her observations were echoed by James, another Black software developer who encountered significant hurdles in securing a position. James's career beginning was marred by the industry-standard practice of whiteboarding during interviews, a process he found not only stressful but also skewed aggressively toward abstract theoretical knowledge that is typically emphasized in the curricula of elite schools. "The whiteboard sessions felt like an endurance test, designed to favor those groomed in a very specific educational ethos," Marcus reflected. This method of evaluating candidates disproportionately disadvantages those from more diverse educational backgrounds, not because they lack the requisite knowledge or skills, but because the format itself is exclusionary, prioritizing a narrow band of experiences and problem-solving approaches.

Under a guise of meritocracy, the tech industry's reliance on elite networks for recruitment further exacerbates disparities. Companies often scout talent from a narrow pool of prestigious universities or through referrals, perpetuating a cycle in which the same privileged demographics continue to dominate. Such hiring sidelines applicants from community colleges, Historically Black Colleges and Universities (HBCUs), and Hispanic-Serving Institutions (HSIs), which are often perceived as less prestigious. This approach not only narrows the diversity of thought and experience but also reinforces the idea that only those from certain backgrounds are fit for success.[4]

The hiring of software developers, while ostensibly based on objective, meritocratic criteria, frequently hinges on the subjective notion of "culture fit." This criterion tends to favor candidates who reflect the current workforce's demographics, social and cultural backgrounds, and perspectives. As a result, culture fit reinforces existing racial and gender hierarchies within tech organizations. It relies on racialized and gendered social networks, with employees informally encouraged to recommend friends or former colleagues for open positions. Such recommendations are often given priority or special consideration during the hiring process, perpetuating a cycle of similarity and exclusion.[5]

Despite these disparities, tech companies frequently justify their hiring practices by asserting a perceived shortage of tech talent among underrepresented groups. They argue that the available pool of qualified candidates from these demographics simply isn't large enough to fulfill their recruitment quotas, compelling them to default to their established networks and preferred elite institutions. This rationale conveniently sidesteps the systemic barriers that obstruct access to opportunities for Black software developers and other marginalized groups. By attributing the diversity gap to an alleged scarcity of talent, rather than confronting the industry's complicity in maintaining this imbalance, tech companies perpetuate a narrative that deflects responsibility.[6]

The employment numbers for underrepresented groups, particularly in technical roles, remain stubbornly low. This issue transcends mere underrepresentation; it signals a deeper, more systemic problem of exploitation and exclusion in the hiring of Black software developers and other marginalized demographics. Many individuals from these groups are relegated to lower-level, precarious positions, offering scant chances for career advancement or stable employment.

Hired into Precarity

Eliza, a twenty-eight-year-old Black front-end web developer from New York City, works at a tech company based in Manhattan. Despite a seemingly lucrative package of a near six-figure salary and stock options, her career feels fraught with uncertainty. "The ground beneath me always feels like it's shifting," Eliza said. "I'm constantly learning, not just to advance, but to simply keep pace." Such rapid change also directly affects her work. Eliza's career faced an abrupt disruption during the layoffs that swept through the tech industry in February 2023, following the easing of the COVID-19 pandemic. "Despite all my hard work, my sense of security is an illusion," Eliza reflected.[7]

These layoffs disproportionately affected marginalized groups. "Halting DEI [diversity, equity, and inclusion] efforts might seem like a quick fix," Eliza pointed out, "but the long-term damage to employee diversity can be far-reaching." Eliza observed that, following layoffs that disproportionately affected DEI initiatives, employees of color found themselves shouldering the responsibility for tasks once managed by dedicated teams. This shift forced Black and Latine tech workers to engage in unpaid "equity work," efforts aimed at fostering a more inclusive workplace culture.[8]

Yet Eliza confronts not only the volatility of layoffs and the insecurity of temporary positions but also the profound sense of isolation as a woman of color. "It's not just about job security; it's also about constantly feeling overlooked," she shared. Eliza's experience highlights a disheartening trend: a lack of support for personal and professional growth. "The companies I've worked with talk about growth, but it seems to apply to everyone but us," she observed. Over her decade-long journey in front-end development, Eliza has consistently observed a stark contrast in how mentorship and growth opportunities are allocated. "My Black colleagues and I watch as others are groomed for success," she said, "while we're left to fend for ourselves."

Black and Latine software developers often find themselves at a disadvantage due to limited mentoring opportunities from managers, who typically belong to more dominant racial groups. This lack of support and guidance significantly hampers Black and Latine software developers' professional development and narrows their path to promotions and broader professional networks. "I've had management refuse to give me more challenging work, even if it was the subject I was passionate about," said Khadija, a thirty-year-old Black software developer. "Instead, they prefer to mentor someone else with far less experience in that area to undertake the job." This practice not only demoralizes motivated and capable developers such as Khadija but also perpetuates the cycle of exclusion and inequality.

Marcus, a thirty-year-old Black software developer from a working-class background in Detroit, shared insights into the experiences of several Black colleagues regarding their end-of-year evaluations. These evaluations were notably devoid of constructive feedback, a situation that Marcus found troubling. He recounted, "Managers would assert that they weren't performing their duties adequately yet failed to provide clear explanations or guidance on what exactly was lacking. Rather than offering feedback, they resorted to vague critiques, suggesting a lack of motivation or that my colleagues were not keeping pace with the latest technological advancements." This approach not only left the employees in question without a clear path to improvement but also highlighted a systemic issue within the company culture: a tendency to attribute performance issues to personal failings rather than identifying and addressing specific areas for professional development.[9]

The lived experience of tech company culture for Black software developers is marked by a paradoxical heightened visibility, despite their underrepresentation. This visibility subjects employees of color to undue pressure to conform to conventional standards of "professionalism" while simultaneously casting them as perpetual outsiders within their workplace environments. "You can't just show up to your work dressed casually like some guys get away with," Shawn, a twenty-four-year-old Black male software developer, explained. "A white or Asian dude in a hoodie is a nerd. A Black person wearing a hoodie is an outsider." Shawn's experiences reveal the intersection of race and gender. For Black men, failure to look sharp and conform to racialized and gendered depictions of professionalism means exposure to negative stereotypes of Black masculinity.[10]

But wearing a suit, for example—the dressing norm in the corporate workspace to show one's group membership and status—presents an extra challenge. A business suit distances Black men from looking like "nerds," while white and Asian workers can unproblematically dress casually and be recognized as technologists and software developers. Aware of these perceptions, Black software developers must constantly be aware of their surroundings and how they present themselves to their colleagues. To be seen as a software developer, and not as a salesperson or human resources (HR) employee, for example, Shawn frequently wore shirts with slogans that legitimated his presence in the office in addition to claiming membership to the professional group he belonged to. "I wore shirts that had 'Black Code Rules' or 'Black Nerd' written on them," he said.[11]

The hypervisibility that Black men and women experience was described by some of my respondents as exhausting. Even when she engaged in constant code-switching—the process of shifting from one language or dialect to another to be taken more seriously in professional or other conversational settings—Diana, the twenty-seven-year-old Black woman mentioned in the Introduction, was still not included as a member of the workplace. She said:

One of the biggest things that bothers me at my job is how people behave around me. As a person of my color, there's not many of us. I try to be as friendly as I possibly can. This means a lot of code-switching—changing your tone of voice to fit in—and that's not something I like to do. It's something that bothers me. To be able to have to do it, in order to talk to somebody. Many times, people do not even acknowledge that I'm there—not even as a coder; I'm talking, as a human being. I have felt alone most of the time. The only time I talk to people is when we have team meetings. I am trying to be friendly and approachable. I try to do that, so people say hello to you. People would not even make eye contact with me. But you see me, and then when you come close to me you look the other way. So, it's hard for me to deal with that and get back to work, when I'm thinking about what just happened.

The ability to become "invisible" within, a privilege often enjoyed by white and Asian colleagues, starkly eludes Black and Latine software developers. For employees from these racialized groups, their presence in the workplace is conspicuously marked, subjecting them to assumptions and biases that undermine their professional identity. This discrepancy in experience between white employees, who can present themselves purely as individuals, and their Black and Latine colleagues, who are often seen through the lens of racial stereotypes, starkly illustrates the pervasive influence of race in determining who feels included or alienated at work. Reflecting on her experiences, Monique, who was thirty-one, shared, "I can never just be a *software developer*. I can never blend into the crowd. A Black person in the office? They must be delivering something, or work in sales, at best. But a geek? . . . [N]ever. . . . [T]hat just does not register in people's minds."

Despite promises to bring well-paid software jobs to New York City's ethnically and racially diverse population, many workers are not benefiting from the growth of the high-tech economy. Employment gains for Black and Latine workers at companies such as Amazon, Google, and Facebook are usually concentrated in low-status departments such as information technology (IT) support, sales, human resources, marketing, and communication. Software development remains predominantly a space for white and Asian men. This segregation is confirmed by the demographic data released by some technology firms. What makes such segregation resistant to change is the dominant culture of tech companies, which suppresses interrogations of racism and discrimination in the workplace and the organization in general.[12]

A Culture of Inequality

"What takes place in the office never gets out there. HR doesn't really do anything; you just accept it, or you quit," explained Sara, a twenty-nine-year-old Black software developer who has worked in this field since 2015. Employees who speak about discrimination are ignored or even face retaliation for addressing the injustice in the companies they work for. Stringent nondisclosure agreements (NDAs) protect employers and further disadvantage employees by forbidding them to share publicly their experiences in the workplace. Moreover, preferential treatment in the form of light penalties privileges some workers more than others. "I feel dudes who have never worked with Black people and women in particular get a light slap on the wrist if they say racist stuff or show racist memes during lunch breaks," Sara says. "I feel HR continuously protects the workers it deems more valuable."[13]

Sara's experience was echoed by Leslie Miley, former director of engineering at Slack, who spoke during the panel "Surviving and Thriving (while Black) in Tech" at a conference in 2019. Miley, who has held numerous leadership positions at Twitter, Google, and Apple, highlighted tech's persistent negligence when it comes to DEI, despite symbolic actions of goodwill, and criticized its exclusionary work culture. "When it comes to tech, company [financial] valuations are more important than [moral] values," he stated. Miley's comment refers to how investors and tech chief executives place more emphasis on attaining the highest financial valuation for their companies than on creating a safe workspace for employees. For Miley, this was far from a small issue; it characterizes all successful tech companies nationwide.[14]

Miley accused some of tech's most highly valued software developers-turned-entrepreneurs of receiving millions in venture funding despite blatantly expressing problematic ideologies and ignoring toxic work environments. For example, Palmer Luckey, the founder of Oculus and a software developer-turned-billionaire, received numerous rounds of venture capital funding despite promoting racist and sexist views. After many years of ignoring his divisive rhetoric, Luckey was fired by Facebook in 2016 for having contributed to an anti–Hillary Clinton political action committee and allying himself with moderators of the notoriously racist pro–Donald Trump forum r/The_Donald and posting racist memes on Reddit under the pseudonym "NimbleRichMan." Yet as a successful entrepreneur, he continues to receive massive amounts of funding from venture capitalists.[15]

When discussing the broader tech culture and its intersection with racial inequality, several of my respondents shared that encountering colleagues who share viewpoints similar to those of Luckey is a regular aspect of their professional lives. "Many software developers I worked with look up to these people. For them, work is all about their code and the value of their stock options. Nothing else matters," said Bobby, a twenty-nine-year-old Black software developer who grew up in Brooklyn and secured a scholarship to study computer science at a prestigious private university. He found himself surrounded by other computer science graduates from elite colleges when he started working for tech companies in New York City. At his first job, he was the only Black person in a team of fifteen composed exclusively of white and Asian male software developers, both U.S.-born and foreign. "I was a unicorn," Bobby said. "I had a [computer science] degree from a top university; I was one of the best coders on my team; *and* I was Black." Bobby's status ostracized him even more from the work environment of his company. His extreme visibility as a Black software developer exposed him to stereotypes that his colleagues expressed to evaluate his success:

> My colleagues would tell me that I am one of the "smart ones." That I should be a manager and "lead the way." That was their way of sympathizing with me—by justifying my success on the basis of *their* understanding of intelligence. They would give me their unsolicited opinions about how "others" could have made it to where I am had they made the right choices and adopted "smart" approaches to work.

After almost ten years of working in tech, Bobby decided to quit working for tech companies. He began working on his own company, which designed digital educational tools for low-income teenagers interested in learning how to write computer code. Why he quit was something I had the opportunity to ask him when we met for a second interview by video chat in the spring of 2021. He said:

> There was no sense of community at the companies I worked for. When I worked as a product optimization engineer, management would dictate to our team that the priority was to

make the product better, make the website perform better. I kept asking myself. Better for who? Who is really benefiting from this? That is something I wrestled with a lot in my career working for big tech. I always felt there were bigger issues in front of us. I do not believe in this fairy tale that "we need to grow as much as possible." I could not see how my people would benefit from a "great" online interface. So I decided to use my skills to build something different.

Similar to Bobby, Matthew, a thirty-three-year-old Black man, expressed his disagreement with the values that tech companies prioritize. Unlike Bobby, Matthew continues to work for a big tech company, but he also expressed his disagreement with company culture and understood why many people become disillusioned when working for tech companies:

> I see a paradox in tech. Software developers are pushed by a curiosity—about new technologies, about research, about building things, about expanding knowledge, about changing the world. . . . But you have technological change that pushes new products into the market. I feel companies, employees, and clients get caught into this vortex where we are developing too fast. We are forgetting about what makes us human. For me, the question is always: "Why are we doing this?" I always ask myself that. Why are we recommending this approach? Why are we working on this specific product? We do not even think about what is underlying about the technology. People are just blindly building and perpetuating inequalities.

Other respondents' accounts highlighted cultural discrepancies not at the level of organizational values but among colleagues. Even when Black and Latine employees join the highest echelons of tech companies as successful software developers, they face obstacles in fitting into the culture of their workplace. Maria, a twenty-five-year-old Black software developer, also graduated from a private university in New York City. She earns a high salary that allows her to afford a spacious studio apartment in Williamsburg, Brooklyn. Yet she confesses that being a software developer is not something she wants to do for the rest of her life. Maria is not only distrustful of how secure her job is, but she frequently feels out of place working in tech:

> As employees, we do not have a say in the decision-making process when it comes to the company culture and how that connects to our mental well-being. I struggle a lot at my company. People have high expectations of me, but they do not know how it is to be like me. I am not asking these people to know me, but just for them to be more understanding. I feel like people don't respect that. They just do not see me as who I am.

Similarly, Victoria, a twenty-five-year-old Black woman who works for a large media company building online tools for better news reporting, explained how she doesn't fit the greater tech culture:

> I feel out of place sometimes. First, it's the type of work. A lot of software developers pretend that they are working on amazing projects. Nope. Most of the time you are working on a very small part of a larger project. As a software developer at a large company, you are always a small cog in the machine, doing something that does not really contribute to the greater good. Then there is the other thing about my work that I dislike. After the working day, we are pressured to participate in activities. For example, happy hours are necessary for "team building," according to my manager. At these events I realize that I don't have anything in common with my colleagues. I cannot relate to their hobbies, how they see the world. I work in a very white environment.

The concept of meritocracy was frequently mentioned by respondents. Tech industry spokespeople often tout meritocracy as creating a "race-neutral" environment where passion for hard work and technology unites talented individuals. Historically, proponents have argued that meritocracy renders the tech industry uniquely equitable, even claiming that it is "less racist" than the broader society. This belief persists, as evidenced by my interview with Wesley, a thirty-two-year-old white man, who said: "Racism is, unfortunately, a universal issue. However, in my experience, when you bring talented engineers together, their last concern is race. My colleagues and I, engineers from diverse corners of the globe, concentrate solely on our work. We refuse to let prejudices hinder our problem-solving abilities."[16]

I showed this quote to Sara, the Black software developer quoted at the start of this chapter. "Just because someone is technically skilled or educated, that doesn't mean they cannot be racist," she responded. Moreover, as she explained to me, merit is a not as neutral a principle as people assume. "Merit," in the context of tech, is understood as superior technical knowledge or experience, attained through formal education and training. Sara said that tech companies need to reconfigure what they understand by *merit* before they use it as a justification for the distribution of resources, such as employment and salaries.

Requirements for obtaining a job, mentorship, and career advancement opportunities are more often a result of arbitrary judgment based on biases than a comprehensive standard. The power of meritocracy lies in its entanglement with racial privilege that has allowed certain employees to be chosen for jobs and career advancement through personal connections, recruiting preferences, or other means. Such discriminatory mechanisms become hidden behind a veil of "qualifications," "credentials," and "merit." Meritocracy, perceived as a fair system, has allowed tech companies to ignore underlying structural issues, shielding them from blame. On the contrary, blame is transferred to the worker, arguing that racial disparities are a result of candidates' shortcomings. Addressing the racism embedded in the business practices of tech corporations may be the biggest obstacle in creating a more diverse workforce. Yet an additional barrier exists that contributes to precarity for workers: age discrimination.[17]

5

"Too Old" to Code

Christina is a fifty-five-year-old white woman who works as a full-stack web developer building background components of digital applications and designing interfaces that customers use. She worked as a graphic designer for a New York fashion magazine till the early 2000s but was laid off after the dot-com bubble burst. The shift from print media to digital platforms forced her to look for another job. While pursuing freelance gigs as a photographer, Christina returned to college and graduated in 2011 with a degree in computer science. This would have been her second degree after graduating with a bachelor of arts in graphic design in 1993. Like many in her age cohort, she saw more opportunity in working for the tech industry.

At forty and with high hopes, she started applying for jobs in New York City. After being rejected by several companies, she was told that she didn't meet their "technical requirements." Most companies did not even call her back. Christina became convinced that the technical skills she learned in college were not up to par with the digital economy's requirements. To gain more insight and learn the latest technologies, she started visiting tech meetups. This exposed her to a new reality. It was 2015, and the heavily infused theoretical curriculum she had studied at college did not prepare her for the rapidly evolving, product-centered technologies. According to Christina, programming languages such as C and PHP are useful, but "they simply do not address practical problems or offer the latest product solutions." Without an understanding, for example, of Node.js, a JavaScript paradigm that most start-ups and companies use, Christina was out of luck.

After engaging in an intense period of self-learning, following crash courses in JavaScript, front-end development, and back-end frameworks, Christina started marketing herself as a full-stack developer, capable of building and executing new features without having to coordinate with a team of developers. When I interviewed Christina in the summer of 2023, the year she turned fifty-four, she had still not landed a full-time job and was employed on a temporary contract at a firm. She complained that there were no entry-level jobs for people her age, despite the fact that she was proficient in several programming languages and frameworks considered cutting-edge. Moreover, more than a decade older than the median age for software professionals, she felt excluded.

Senior software developers deemed "too old" confront heightened precarity compared with their younger counterparts. They encounter employment barriers due to perceptions of being costlier to hire and retain. Seniority and expertise, instead of being valued assets, are at times seen as hindrances to lean operation and rapid innovation. The relentless pace of change pushes senior workers to increased burnout, as they must continuously adapt to evolving technological demands, which foster anxiety about potential replacement by younger "talent." Finally, exclusionary work environments that see the "ideal worker" as male, white, and younger than thirty-five often lead to senior software developers feeling marginalized as less adaptable, more expensive, and ill-suited to a company's youthful culture.

Seniority in an Era of Innovation

When Mark Zuckerberg was twenty-two, he spoke in front of students at a Stanford University start-up event. "Young people are just smarter," he said with a straight face. "Why are most chess masters under thirty? Young people just have simpler lives. We may not own a car; we may not own a family." Zuckerberg was famous for frequently instituting hackathons—coding competitions—at Facebook, pushing employees to conceive of and complete a project over a night of intense coding. The movie *The Social Network* portrays one of these hackathons at an early stage of Facebook's growth, when Zuckerberg was still a student at Harvard. During a famous recruiting scene, college students were expected to solve a coding program in less than a few minutes while taking shots of strong liquor. The idea that hackathons foster innovation through exuberant and concentrated bursts of creativity and ingenuity is what Zuckerberg defended as the personality of Facebook, the ability to "build something really good in a night." Such behavior is promoted by a corporate culture that celebrates innovation through "youth," something that is passed to individuals through socialization.[1]

In the past several years, reports have shown that IBM fired more than 100,000 employees to improve its corporate image for millennials. A lot of the terminated workers were stereotyped as old, outdated, and harmful to the new image IBM wanted to present to the world. As the company's former vice president of human resources admitted, IBM wanted to position itself as a "cool, trendy organization rather than an old fuddy-duddy organization." Just like other major tech companies, IBM has been accused of promoting a company culture that is better suited to the lifestyles of young employees who can afford to work longer hours, take risks, and innovate through socialization and play. At these companies, the job of software developer is being associated with a "youthful" environment where fast-paced innovation, rapid deployment of code, and overly long working hours are the requirements of the ideal worker.[2]

Despite the commonly held view that programming skills often improve with age, extending well into an individual's fifties and sixties, this correlation is frequently dismissed by management and younger colleagues. Consequently, senior workers face derogatory stereotypes, such as being deemed "out of touch" with the latest technologies or lacking adaptability, which undermines the respect and recognition their experience warrants. This environment fosters a culture in which their contributions are undervalued and their expertise is questioned. "You're constantly battling the notion that you can't possibly understand the newest frameworks or programming languages because of your age," said Jordan, a fifty-eight-year-old software developer. "It's as if your decades of solving complex problems count for nothing the moment a new coding language appears on the scene."

Kevin, a forty-year-old Asian American front-end web developer at Amazon, described a prevailing generational divide at his workplace, noting that interactions between senior and junior software developers are often marked by tension. He attributed this schism to several factors, including the competitive nature of the tech environment and the substantial salaries that young professionals, often in their early twenties, command:

> At my company, you have some kids that come straight out of college. They are in their early twenties, and make $160K, first salary, and living in New York City. The culture of some of these companies enables their behavior. They think they are on this golden path, where life is easy, and when they see older people struggling, they ask themselves, naïvely, "Why are people struggling like that?" I have seen a lot of people my age disrespected by younger know-it-alls.

Aside from stereotypes associated with age, corporate strategies compound this problem. New technological requirements have transformed how tech companies value an employee's technical skill set. Until recently, labor markets were characterized by a skill bias: Technology firms favored workers with more skill relative to those with less. Yet senior software developers who supposedly possess more technical skills as a result of their longer tenure are being pushed out of the labor force because their skills are deemed obsolete. For example, a fifty-year-old programmer may have acquired knowledge of several programming languages over the course of their career but may not yet be familiar with the latest variation of "hot" technological tools in demand, such as React (JavaScript). While a junior developer might lack the rich and detailed knowledge about software development that a senior developer possesses, they will know the latest programs and thus be a more suitable, as well as a cheaper, hire.

The rapid evolution of the tech industry necessitates a workforce that is not only proficient but also constantly updated with the newest technological trends. In an industry that often associates youth with innovation and flexibility, senior employees must constantly refine their skills to stay competitive. A unique challenge emerges: Workers must leverage their depth of experience while remaining adaptable to the ever-changing technological landscape. Corey, a forty-six-year-old Asian American software developer, explained that senior workers, just like their younger colleagues, are expected to grow continuously as experts and embrace a flexible work orientation:

> Technologies are changing almost daily. At some point, you will have to go and learn some new skills. For example, you will *have* to learn React at some point. You might be, like, "Screw it. I have ten to twenty years of experience in front-end developing. I'm not going to learn this." But it's probably not a good idea. You need to match the hunger that the younger developers have, participate in new projects, learn new skills.

In tech management, a prevalent strategy involves replacing individual contributors or entire teams when software developers show reluctance to adopt new technologies. Such a practice underlines a stark reality in which the pursuit of the latest technological advancements often eclipses the value placed on loyalty and depth of accumulated experience. Hesitance to adapt swiftly is often perceived as resistance to progress, inadvertently marking a professional's expertise as outdated. The industry's preference for innovation over the valuable perspectives of seasoned professionals places these experienced workers at a disadvantage.

Matthew, a fifty-year-old white man, has managed engineering teams for the past fifteen years. He explained that teams who "resist" innovation by refusing to adapt to technological change are often replaced by new teams willing to use the tools dictated by management and the market.[3] "When we hit our upper limit, we try to change the technology we are working on," he said. "But I've seen it time and time again. Developers don't want to embrace new technologies. So what does the business do? It finally gets fed up and fires the team and brings in a new team, so what you see is this turnover of entire teams." The threat of replacement not only sidelines seasoned professionals but also instills a culture of fear and disposability, undermining the value of accumulated knowledge and the nuanced understanding that comes with years of hands-on problem solving. "It feels like you're constantly running on a treadmill that's speeding up: Miss a step, and you're off," reflected Corey. "The industry's relentless pursuit of the new often overlooks the depth of insight and stability experienced workers bring to the table."

Floriana, a forty-seven-year-old white woman, is one of the software developers who experienced how workers are affected by management's decisions. When she started working as a software developer in the mid-1990s, she witnessed how workers in their fifties were being pressured by management into early retirement. "Perhaps I was too overconfident to really understand their problem, but I know exactly how it feels now," Floriana said. "It is almost impossible for developers to keep up with the fast tempo set by predominantly young managers." During a meeting while working for her previous company, she was asked to "drop everything" and change technology stack. For her, it was clear that management wanted to replace her:

> When companies want to save on costs, they pressure management to hire an excited but also desperate college graduate who is willing to take half your salary and work twenty-hour days. That or simply outsource the project. Management wants us to switch projects, technologies, customers. They don't see how this is unsustainable. Instead of investing in actual growth, they treat us like we are expendable. It's impossible to switch every year and remain knowledgeable of your skill set.

For Dimitri, a fifty-two-year-old self-taught software developer from Russia, technologies are being changed dramatically with no regard for the people who still support what management calls "obscure" technologies. For him, the problem is not necessarily technological change but the sudden changes made by management that cause the replacement of senior employees who are costlier:

> They make fun of my team because we use Microsoft's ASP.
> NET. They want us to transition to Django, for example. I am
> not opposed to this change. It's not going to be too hard to
> switch for me because I know Python. But what is next? How
> long till the next switch? Every time these switches happen, the
> oldest employees are the first to go because they are the highest
> wage earners. I am worried about some of them. Companies no
> longer need fifteen developers to do the job.

While Dimitri is confident in his ability to adapt, he poses broader questions about the relentless cycle of technological shifts. This sector is known for its abrupt changes, often dictated by management in response to new technological advancements and market demands. These shifts frequently align with the perception that senior, more set-in-their-ways employees hinder innovation, leading to a worrying pattern: With each update, the more senior, higher-salaried employees are often the first to be dismissed.

Rapid innovation not only leads to job insecurity. It also cultivates an intensely competitive atmosphere among team members. Individuals feel compelled to prove their worth in a sector that values innovation over experience, contributing to an exhausting reality. As Dimitri put it: "You're expected to collaborate, yet you can't shake the feeling that your colleague might soon take your place." This dynamic not only strains relationships among workers but also hampers efforts to organize. The focus on individual survival and competition dilutes the collective drive for unionization as finding common ground in shared struggles becomes increasingly challenging.

Many senior software developers, keenly aware of the precarious nature of their employment, are compelled to spend additional hours outside their standard work hours to enhance their skills. This dedication to ongoing professional growth stems from the desire to remain competitive and, ideally, a step ahead of younger colleagues. Software developers must predict or speculate on market trends to maintain an edge on their peers, mirroring the strategic foresight often associated with finance investors. "Navigating the tech industry feels like being a day trader, where your investments are in your own skills," Aarav, a forty-four-year-old software developer, explained. "If I learn something that's new and hot and changing all the time, then I can maybe have an advantage over someone who's not so interested in studying after work."

For software developers such as Harry, a forty-year-old white man who worked for a security firm, the essence of their role inherently involves embracing new technologies. "Being inquisitive and identifying flaws in old frameworks is central to a software developer's job," Harry noted. "Continuous learning isn't optional in this field." However, many of my interviewees view self-directed learning as a way for tech companies to shift the responsibility for training onto the employees themselves rather than providing formal training opportunities. One respondent expressed the challenge of balancing work and learning: "I have no time, and my learning rate has decreased significantly. The only way to learn something is at work. Someone at work suggested we upgrade to a new stack, and everybody learned it and got invested in it. And I said, 'Yeah, because if we do it at work, that's the only way I'll do it; I'm not going to do it at home!'"

Yet for workers with family commitments who cannot spare additional hours after work, this expectation becomes a daunting obligation. Most do not have the chance to explore new technologies during office hours through hands-on projects. Consequently, for many, updating their skills with new libraries and technology stacks becomes a mandatory post-work activity. This shifts the burden onto the individuals themselves, making them responsible for their own upskilling—tasks previously managed by employers.

The incessant drive to learn becomes particularly challenging for women, mothers, or those who want to become mothers—those with families, as they grapple with the pressing need to balance their professional development with their familial responsibilities. Striking this equilibrium can prove arduous, as they are often unable to afford the luxury of blurring the boundaries between work and leisure that their younger colleagues might enjoy.

Coding and Caregiving

> Throughout my twelve-year tenure in the industry, I have yet to encounter a mother who is actively working as a software developer. Among the few older women software developers whom I admire as role models, all are without children. While I've worked alongside numerous fathers, I've never had the opportunity to work with a pregnant colleague during our time working together.
> —Esther

Esther, a thirty-eight-year-old Asian American software developer, sheds light on the tech industry's biases against age and gender, especially concerning motherhood. Female software developers often face pressure to delay starting a family, typically until their early thirties or beyond, a decision that places them at a disadvantage in terms of age. At many tech firms, the prime years for career advancement overlap with those traditionally viewed as best for childbearing. The industry's preference for youth, underscored by a culture that prizes rapid innovation and extensive work hours, creates additional hurdles for those contemplating parenthood. Consequently, women who opt for motherhood later in life face skepticism regarding their dedication or their ability to manage demanding roles while raising a family—a scrutiny seldom applied to their younger or male colleagues.

The challenges for women often start with maternity leave. Despite some companies' gaining attention for their generous parental leave policies, many mothers find themselves facing the stigma of using time off. When they return to work, women often face hostility, with their absence viewed as a lapse in their commitment and productivity. Karen, who became a mother after ascending to the role of senior software developer, returned from maternity leave only to discover she had been passed over for a significant project. "Upon my return, I found that my coworkers and managers—all of whom are men—interpreted my leave to care for my child as a negative career move and indicative of a lack of commitment to technology," she explained. "They expected me to immediately resume full productivity, with no consideration for my need to gradually reintegrate into the workforce or to adjust to my new personal responsibilities."

Upon returning from maternity leave, mothers frequently find themselves perceived as having obsolete or outdated skills. This perception forced Daphne, a fifty-year-old white woman, essentially to restart her career in a different direction: "I reentered the workforce at age forty-six, once my children were old enough. Despite my efforts to update my skills, they were, unfortunately, still considered outdated." Many mothers opt for contract work, choosing forty-hour-per-week contracts that better accommodate the responsibilities of parenthood. However, the drawback is that these positions often offer lower pay and lack predictability. "It can be desert out there," Anne, forty-three and Asian, commented, noting the trend among companies to hire more affordable software developers from overseas. "Gig work, while flexible, can be exceedingly demanding and exhausting," she said. "Balancing childcare, a forty-hour workload, and dealing with clients who see you as expendable has led me to a point of severe burnout."

The biases surrounding maternity leave are further exacerbated by the male-dominated culture in the tech industry that not only cultivates a sense of isolation among women but also creates implicit barriers to their career advancement. In such an environment, where late-night work sessions and an unyielding work ethic are glorified, mothers striving for balance between work and family life frequently find themselves marginalized. "The 'best employees' are seen as the unattached twenty-year-old men ripe for burnout. I find myself at a crossroads, contemplating whether sacrificing my career is the price of starting a family. Regrettably, I'm leaning toward the realization that tech has no room for mothers," said Xiaoxia, a thirty-five-year-old Asian woman, highlighting the stark choice many women feel they must make between career and family.

The intensity of technological change, coupled with the expectation one will work extended hours, means that mothers often find themselves in a relentless cycle of juggling project deadlines with childcare—a balance that is both exhausting and unsustainable.

"Given the rapid pace of change in our field, even a brief hiatus of six months to a year can render one's skills and knowledge obsolete, severely hindering career advancement," Anastasia, a thirty-seven-year-old Latina, pointed out. "This causes a troubling dilemma between family and career, leading many potential mothers to exit the profession altogether."

Martha, a fifty-year-old Black software developer, highlighted a concerning trend despite recent diversity initiatives. These efforts have led to an increase in the recruitment of younger women as junior software developers. However, Martha pointed out a stark disparity at higher levels of the hierarchy: "As you ascend through the ranks and accumulate experience, the presence of senior women diminishes." Martha emphasized the demanding nature of the tech industry, which, in her view, requires nearly all of one's mental focus, leaving minimal energy for personal life. "Tech demands 98 percent of your brainpower. What's left is barely enough for your family life," she elaborated. "I've seen firsthand how the combination of a high-pressure job and a hostile workplace forces many women out of the field, especially as they reach their forties. It's disheartening to witness talented professionals being worn down by the relentless demands of the job and toxic interactions, only to spend their weekends trying to catch up on work."

The adoption of remote work during the pandemic, heralded for introducing flexibility, also presents unique challenges. Blurring the once distinct lines between professional obligations and family life, it often results in prolonged work hours and an unspoken expectation of constant availability. For mothers navigating the complexities of child-rearing alongside their careers, remote work without explicitly defined boundaries and robust policies that support working parents risks perpetuating the very challenges it seeks to mitigate. The blend of work and home environments means mothers may face difficulty carving out uninterrupted time for both work and family responsibilities. "As a mother in tech, remote work has meant my home is now my office, but without clear limits, it feels like there's no off switch. Juggling deadlines and childcare from the same space is a constant balancing act," one software developer and mother shared, highlighting the nuanced struggle of maintaining professionalism and parenthood without the physical separation of an office.

The challenges faced by senior workers—ranging from battling stereotypes associated with maternity leave to navigating the intense demands of both work and family life—are starkly indicative of the broader systemic inequalities at play. However, these issues do not exist in isolation. As we turn our attention to the intersection of race and age, it becomes clear that these dimensions further complicate the landscape of diversity and inclusion within tech.

The Dual Realities of Race and Age

Senior Black software developers often face a dichotomous reality. On one hand, their seniority allows them to assert some level of dominance in a work environment that is highly unequal and racialized. This position can offer a measure of authority and respect that might otherwise be difficult to attain. On the other hand, their senior status also distances them from the youthful image often associated with the ideal tech worker, placing them at odds with the industry's expectations of innovation and agility.

William, forty-eight, is currently a software development manager at a prominent tech company. He climbed the ranks from software developer to senior developer, then team lead, working at various companies along the way. His progression through these roles reflects a solid track record in both programming and team management. Yet his fifteen-year career was marked by consistent efforts to overcome the stereotypes faced by Black men. He said:

> With every career you have certain stereotypes. People think in their minds that certain people should be doing certain things. A true geek wears hoodies, has a scruffy beard, [and] drinks soda and codes all day. We used to do casual Fridays, and instead of wearing my usual outfit, I would come to work with sneakers and a hoodie. The looks I would get were crazy. Some people would mistake me for a janitor or a "kid" that was delivering something. . . . That was the end of casual Fridays for me.

Now, as a manager, William emphasizes the importance of appearing older and more seasoned. Adopting a more senior demeanor is crucial for gaining respect and being taken seriously in the workplace, especially as a Black man. Yet his choice of attire also has consequences for how he is perceived as software developer. "When I wear a suit, I am no longer seen as a software developer," he said. "So you can't really win."

William's experiences highlight the complex interplay among race, appearance, and professional identity in tech. On one hand, dressing in a way that conveys seniority and authority can help him counteract some of the racial bias he faces, providing a visual cue that aligns with traditional notions of leadership. However, the tech industry often champions a more casual dress code that is associated with youthfulness and technological authenticity. Thus, by dressing more formally, William risks distancing himself from the very qualities that are celebrated in a tech environment, such as being deeply engaged in coding and technical problem solving.

But seniority is not always guaranteed. The experience of Kareem, the forty-eight-year-old Black software developer discussed in the Introduction, illustrates how seniority and experience do not necessarily guarantee that a Black software developer will be taken seriously in the "white space" of the office and be allowed to participate in the decision-making process as an equal. Despite his knowledge of both the financial field and web development, during his twenty-year career Kareem was frequently seen by younger white managers as obstinate and "difficult to deal with." "I would take the initiative, and this threatened other white employees," he said. "I understood that they were not used to having a Black person telling them what to do." Kareem's initiative as a senior employee violated symbolic boundaries that separated Black and white workers; as a result, he was openly ostracized, supposedly because he was "old" and "stubborn."

Disregard for seniority among Black professionals is further exemplified by the experience of Lisa, a seasoned software developer. Despite having more than fifteen years of experience, she often finds herself excluded from crucial meetings and overlooked in conversations about future project directions. "Despite my years of service, I am regularly bypassed in favor of younger, less experienced colleagues when it comes time to voice strategic input," she shared.

Kareem's and Lisa's experiences highlight how racial biases can overshadow the professional achievements and seniority of Black employees. In these environments, being Black and senior does not insulate one from the challenges posed by workplace racism; rather, it can exacerbate them. This occurs because traditional workplace hierarchies and power dynamics are disrupted when Black employees ascend to senior roles. Their white colleagues, unaccustomed to reporting to Black superiors, may react negatively. These reactions are often subtle and manifest as resistance to leadership, questioning of decisions, or exclusion from key discussions, subtly perpetuating a racially charged barrier to genuine inclusion and equality in the workplace.

East Asian men, who form the majority of software developers at several large tech companies, experience a different reality from that of Black men. "Acting young," particularly through casual clothing styles, and openly "nerding out" reinforce their credibility as software developers and allow them to integrate successfully into the company culture. Chen, forty-five, who was born in South Korea but grew up in New York City, works as a software developer for Amazon. "Everyone on my team is really young—like, in their mid-twenties," he told me. "I feel more comfortable dressing young, acting young, so I can look young." Acting young serves not only as a strategy to avoid being seen as outdated or less valuable due to age. It also reinforces racialized perceptions of Asianness. Within this context, youth is often closely associated with Asianness. Asian software developers are stereotypically viewed as "whiz kids" and "prodigies," embodying traits of high achievement, hard work, and academic success.[4]

Kyle, an Asian American man and a senior software developer at forty-eight, has spent decades navigating the stereotypes associated with Asianness. He reported:

> I was always that Asian "kid," terrific at math. As a software developer, especially when I first started working, I experienced favorable treatment in some ways. I was the go-to guy

when someone had messed up their code. Sometimes I didn't know what was wrong, but I just went with it, you know what I mean? But when you get older, and the stereotypes about "Asians never aging" stop, you are no longer that kid who rules. You become that two-hundred-year-old dude that still codes.

According to Kyle, young Asian workers are more susceptible than their young white peers to exploitation and being overworked in the office. Stereotypical assumptions about their energy levels and stamina can lead managers and coworkers sometimes to take advantage of them. But once a worker crosses the boundary of being "young," their ability as a coder is questioned and their value as a worker decreases. This shift not only impacts their day-to-day work but also their long-term career trajectory, challenging the initial advantages they might have experienced.

Technological innovation focuses on the future, not the past. Its strength lies in how it evolves and changes; how it pushes forward. But who are the protagonists of the future? It appears that they are the "younger generation." As we saw, Zuckerberg said that young people are "just smarter." Although he would probably not utter those exact same words today—now that he is "older"—he probably still believes that employees in their twenties, with more excitement and fewer distractions, are the ideal workers for his company.

Age discrimination often goes unchallenged, reflecting deep-seated biases within the tech industry. Senior software developers are frequently seen as obstacles to innovation, stereotyped as less "tech-savvy" than their younger counterparts and considered costlier by management. Instead of being valued as an asset, their extensive experience is often viewed as a barrier to entry. Consequently, senior workers' job applications are disproportionately filtered out based on perceived "culture fit" issues. Despite the industry's rhetoric of meritocracy, which claims to prioritize skill and experience, senior workers are often dismissed as the least qualified candidates for software development roles.

Senior workers face considerably more challenges with precarious employment forms than their younger colleagues. They endure higher levels of stress and anxiety about job security, worrying about the stability of their careers, which can significantly impact their sense of self-worth. In addition, they are frequently excluded from career development programs that are typically designed to help younger workers ascend the corporate ladder, leaving them with fewer opportunities for advancement. Moreover, senior workers often experience isolation at work and are the targets of age-related remarks and microaggressions. Unfortunately, their seniority, rather than protecting them from the precarious conditions of the new economy, often exacerbates their vulnerability.

The prevailing ideologies of meritocracy, individualism, and innovation that dominate the tech industry often obscure the diverse experiences of precarity faced by workers from various demographics. In the next chapter, I explore strategies for dismantling these beliefs and fostering unity among workers across these divides. By banding together, workers can not only confront discriminatory practices but also advocate for structural changes that support all workers, regardless of age or race, and help break down the organizational and ideological barriers that perpetuate inequality.

6

Tech Workers Unite!

I work in a fast-paced industry, so unions are antithetical
to the spirit of innovation. Our ethos is built on the freedom
to explore, to fail and learn, and to pivot without barriers
or constraints.
—Paul

Paul, a forty-year-old senior software developer, met with me at a café near his office on a Tuesday at 7 P.M. As he ordered coffee, he glanced at the large clock behind the counter. "I only have thirty minutes," he said, citing a looming deadline and the hectic pace at work. Although Paul enjoys working as a software developer, he shared several grievances about his job. His primary issue was with management, whom he found irrational, lacking the engineering mindset that he brings to his work and often making unreasonable last-minute changes. This, he explained, disrupts workflow continuity and contributes to a work environment that is both chaotic and exhausting.

Paul is also conscious of being "too old" in an industry that favors youth. He meticulously shaves every day and trims his sideburns, which are showing white hairs—a change he meets with humor, noting that some of his peers resort to dyeing their hair to appear younger. Aspiring to transition into a managerial role, Paul recognizes the challenges that come with such a shift, acknowledging it's not as straightforward as it might seem. Moreover, the threat of layoffs looms large in his mind. He has witnessed numerous colleagues, including those at senior levels, abruptly lose their jobs. This reality has instilled fear in him that any decrease in his performance or pace could jeopardize his position, highlighting the pervasive sense of job insecurity even among experienced, well-compensated employees.

After listening to Paul's concerns, I gently inquired about potential solutions. He mentioned that, thanks to his strong background, he'd been discreetly applying for other positions. Curious, I brought up the possibility of unionizing. The mere suggestion seemed almost taboo, prompting a visibly negative reaction. Paul dismissed unions as outdated. Upon further prompting to elaborate, he reiterated the deep-seated skepticism toward unionization reflected in the quote that opens this chapter.

The belief in innovation, held by both employers and some employees, generates a strong antipathy for union activity. Many of my interviewees who worked in high-earning positions believe that unions incentivize workers to work fewer hours, which challenges the industry's organizational norm of working beyond traditional work time. More strongly, the structured nature of unions, with their regulations and collective bargaining, could hinder the very essence of technological progress. In this view, the freedom to operate without external limitations is seen as essential for pushing the boundaries of technology.[1]

An individualist culture can be found at the center of the tech industry's almost religious adherence to innovation. By championing the notion that merit and individual initiative are the sole drivers of success, companies and digital elites deflect attention from systemic issues such as job security, equitable pay, and fair working conditions. The narrative that positions workers as lone architects of their destiny, constantly adapting to market forces and innovating on their own behalf, creates an environment in which the collective action and shared demands typical of union movements seem incongruent with the industry's ethos.

Although workers are often encouraged to view their roles as personal projects, the reality for many—particularly those on temporary contracts—is starkly different. These workers are acutely aware of hiring barriers, limited career advancement, layoffs, and toxic work environments, resulting in a pervasive desire to leave the field altogether. However, some have come to realize that the solution lies not in adhering to the individualistic culture, but in embracing collective action to address these systemic issues.

Workers Strike Back

One of the smaller scale forms of worker organizing has been the drafting of open letters to management, calling for an end to discriminatory hiring practices. Employees at several major tech companies have used this approach to publicly challenge their employers to live up to their stated commitments to equity. For example, in June 2020, more than 250 Facebook employees signed an open letter to executives criticizing the company's lack of diversity and inclusion efforts. The letter detailed specific grievances regarding the underrepresentation of Black employees in decision-making roles and called for systemic changes in hiring and promotion processes to rectify ongoing racial disparities. This public action underscored the employees' demands for genuine commitment rather than mere rhetorical support for diversity and inclusion.[2]

To combat pay disparities, workers have started sharing salary information with one another, breaking the long-standing taboo against discussing compensation. Employees at several large tech companies have used platforms such as Team Blind, a website where one can anonymously share salary information and discuss workplace issues. This has created a platform where workers can compare their earnings directly with those of their peers. Although this form of resistance may not always result in tangible actions such as successful collective bargaining, it serves as an important step in making workers aware of how employers treat employees. It may also encourage them to reconsider the power of collective bargaining and negotiations.[3]

In recent years, there have been several high-profile walkouts by workers to demand safer workplaces free from discrimination, racism, and harassment. These actions have drawn significant public and media attention, putting pressure on tech companies to improve their policies and practices regarding workplace culture and safety. In November 2018, thousands of Google employees around the world walked out of their offices to protest the company's handling of sexual harassment claims against executives, as well as other contentious issues. This event not only garnered widespread media coverage but also forced Google to review and change its policies on harassment, demonstrating the power of collective action to push for significant organizational changes.[4]

Workers have also mobilized against their companies' engagement in activities perceived as unethical, such as military contracts and collaborations with U.S. Immigration and Customs Enforcement (ICE). Such actions reflect a growing concern among tech workers about the social and ethical implications of their companies' business decisions and the desire to hold employers accountable to higher moral standards. A notable example occurred in 2018 when Microsoft employees protested the company's $19.4 million contract with ICE, which involved providing processing and data services. The employees argued that the company's technology could be used to facilitate the agency's policies of family separation at the border, sparking a broader debate within the company about the ethical considerations of their government contracts.[5]

The murder of George Floyd in 2020 and the subsequent demonstrations around the world to protest police brutality against African Americans had a profound effect on the tech industry. In the same year, employees began speaking out in greater numbers than ever before about racial discrimination in the tech workplace. No longer afraid to face retaliation, they opened up to researchers and the media about their experiences. A notable case that drew wide media attention and signaled a new era in how employees responded to discrimination was the termination of Tinmit Gebru, cohead of an artificial intelligence (AI) ethics research team at Google in December 2020. Gebru, a Black woman, was asked to withdraw from publication an article she had written that criticized the companies' lack of transparency when it came to racial bias in algorithm work. When she refused to do so, she was forced to resign.[6]

Despite the tech industry's historically nonunionized workforce, there have been significant strides toward unionization in recent years. One of the earliest attempts at unionization can be traced back to the 1990s with the Washington Alliance of Technology Workers (WashTech)–Communications Workers of America (CWA) alliance aimed at Microsoft's temporary workers. Despite initial successes in raising awareness about the plight of "perma-temps" who were employed for long durations without receiving the benefits of full-time employees, this effort struggled to achieve lasting change due to legal battles and aggressive counterstrategies by employers. In the early 2000s, efforts by the CWA to unionize workers at IBM were met with similar challenges. The union aimed to address grievances related to job security and offshoring. However, these efforts largely failed due to strong resistance from management and the difficulty of rallying a geographically dispersed workforce that did not experience a unified workplace culture.[7]

There were, however, sporadic early successes. One example was the formation of the Lanetix chapter of the CWA in 2018, in which software developers and other technical staff at the software company Lanetix successfully unionized in response to unfair labor practices. This was a landmark case because it was one of the first instances in which tech workers negotiated for better terms under the banner of a traditional union, although the company responded by firing the union members, leading to legal battles.[8]

The landscape began to change as awareness of workplace issues such as unfair dismissals, discrimination, and unethical workplace practices grew. The unionization of employees at the crowdfunding company Kickstarter in February 2020 marked a significant turning point as Kickstarter became the first well-known tech company to vote successfully for union formation. This success provided a blueprint for other tech workers, demonstrating that unionization was possible in the sector. A year later, the formation of the Alphabet Workers Union (AWU) at Google, despite its focus on advocacy rather than formal bargaining, was another critical step. It signaled to the world that even at companies with entrenched anti-union philosophies, workers could come together to advocate for their rights and ethical practices.[9]

Another significant development occurred in the gaming industry, a tech sector known for intense work hours and precarious contract work. The unionization of Raven Software employees, a subsidiary of Activision Blizzard, in May 2022 highlighted growing solidarity among workers and the push for better working conditions and job security. This move, affiliated with the CWA, is part of a broader trend in the gaming sector of advocating for workers' rights and proper recognition of their contributions.[10]

These recent strides are not just isolated incidents but show us how workers are recognizing the power of collective action in negotiating not only for better pay and benefits but also for respect and ethical treatment in the workplace. This shift is indicative of a deeper transformation within tech, where the myth of the solitary tech genius is being replaced by a recognition of the collective effort that drives the industry. However, resistance from companies remains strong, as many continue to deploy sophisticated strategies to undermine such organizing efforts and maintain control over their workers.

The Corporate Response

Tech companies employ a variety of strategies to discourage union activities or obstruct them outright. This resistance often involves strategic communications to sway employees' opinions, surveillance of union organizers, and targeted layoffs. Google has faced considerable criticism for its approach to managing unionization efforts within its workforce. One tactic the company uses is the termination of employees actively engaged in organizing or advocating for union activities. Such layoffs, often cloaked in various productivity and privacy-related pretexts, have led to accusations that they were primarily motivated by the employees' involvement in labor activism. For example, in 2019 Google fired four employees who were involved in organizing internal protests, claiming they had violated data security policies.[11]

To prevent unionization efforts, tech companies turn to hiring consultancy firms that specialize in anti-union strategies. These firms use communication campaigns that highlight the potential downsides of unionizing, such as dues, the possibility of strikes, and the implementation of rigid work rules that could limit innovation. In 2020, Amazon hired the law firm Morgan Lewis to assist in advising against unionization efforts at its facilities. The firm helped Amazon to craft messages emphasizing the potential consequences of unionizing, such as the cost of union dues and the risk of strikes, which could disrupt operations and impact employees' earnings. Similarly, in 2019 Google hired an anti-union consulting firm to advise management on widespread worker unrest, including accusations of retaliation against organizers of a global walkout and suppression of dissent within the company.[12]

Tech companies have also made changes to internal policies that limit employees' ability to organize, meet, or discuss labor conditions. For example, updates to industry-wide guidelines restrict certain types of workplace gatherings, which could be interpreted as a way to limit union organizing meetings. These actions, while sometimes framed as maintaining company culture or protecting proprietary information, have been criticized by labor activists and legal authorities as methods to suppress legitimate unionization efforts and the rights of workers to organize. A specific instance of this is when Amazon, in 2020, posted job listings for intelligence analysts tasked with monitoring labor organizing threats and union activities. This role included tracking employee activism and was part of Amazon's broader strategy to control discussions about labor conditions, which sparked significant public and legal backlash.[13]

Tech labor organizers encounter formidable obstacles not only from individual tech companies but also from the structural makeup of the entire industry. The tech industry is inherently fragmented due to the vast differences in company sizes and their global operational strategies, which present unique challenges for unionization efforts. For example, the globalization of operations involves outsourcing significant portions of development work and importing cheaper foreign labor, practices that depress wages and dilute attempts at collective action or solidarity across the workforce. The internationalization of software production encourages this trend, undercutting union organizing as companies continuously seek lower labor costs outside their home countries.[14]

The employment structures that predominantly use temporary workers, vendors, and contractors (TVCs) have been another major barrier to unionization in big tech. These workers often lack the protections and benefits afforded to full-time employees. For instance, Google employs more TVCs than full-time employees. However, the TVCs are not entitled to the same benefits, wages, or job security as Google's full-time staff, making it difficult for them to participate in or benefit from collective bargaining.[15]

Despite these obstacles, the momentum for solidarity is growing. Grassroots movements, social media platforms, and informal networks of support continue to emerge, fostering a sense of community and shared purpose among workers worldwide. But the question remains: How can unionization efforts expand to encompass all workers, particularly given the diverse experiences of precarity outlined in this book? In addition, what strategies could tech workers employ to unite more effectively in their pursuit of collective bargaining and improved workplace conditions?

New Solidarities

Uniting the tech workforce will require an approach that recognizes that individuals face multiple, intersecting forms of discrimination and disadvantage that can compound the precarity of their employment situation. Affinity groups, or Employee Resource Groups (ERGs), have emerged within many tech companies as a partial response to these challenges. These groups offer a space for employees with identities or experiences to support one another, advocate for inclusive policies, and foster a sense of community. While the exact number of such groups varies across companies, they are a common feature in large tech organizations and address a range of identities and interests, from race and gender to mental health and parenting.[16]

Although affinity groups are important in establishing a platform for underrepresented workers and contributing to diversity, equity, and inclusion (DEI) ideals, their existence also illustrates a potential challenge to unionization efforts. By addressing specific issues faced by their members, affinity groups can potentially fragment the unified front needed for effective collective bargaining. In addition, the company-sponsored nature of these groups can sometimes limit their ability to forcefully challenge organizational policies. While these groups provide networking and support opportunities, they frequently align closely with company culture by focusing on themes such as leadership within the existing corporate structure rather than pushing for radical changes or addressing deeper systemic inequalities, such as job security, wage disparities, and labor rights.[17]

Tech workers are not isolated professionals but a cohesive workforce confronting common challenges. Understanding this is crucial to transcending traditional boundaries of role, company, and even geography, recognizing that the issues facing one segment of the digital workforce often mirror those faced by others, albeit with unique nuances. Software developers and other tech professionals, regardless of their perceived status or salary, share a commonality with the broader labor force: the experience of precarity in an industry characterized by rapid change and relentless demands for innovation.

Finding common ground in precarity will allow a bottom-up approach or worker-to-worker unionism, which is a notable shift from traditional union methods. This grassroots approach to unionization, driven by the workers themselves, marks a departure from the top-down tactics historically employed by traditional unions. This model is characterized by drives initiated by self-organized workers who also take on roles typically reserved for union staff, such as organizing training. The major promise of this approach is its potential to scale up significantly. This contrasts with what labor organizers refer to as hot-shop organizing, in which workers organically decide to initiate a union drive and may reach out to a union for help but don't start systematic organizing activities, such as persuading skeptical coworkers, before getting staff guidance. Training, if it occurs at all in hot shops, also typically comes from staff. Moreover, while hot-shop organizing often focuses on a single workplace, worker-to-worker union drives aim to organize across an entire company or even a regional industry, showing a difference in scale and scope.[18]

Worker-to-worker unionism offers several advantages, particularly in industries with high turnover rates, such as tech, and where traditional union strategies have faced challenges. By empowering self-organized groups of workers, this approach reduces reliance on union staff, thus lowering barriers to organizing. In addition, leveraging modern digital tools facilitates communication and coordination among employees across expansive networks. Digital platforms such as social media, forums, and online communities play a pivotal role in this process. These platforms provide spaces free from corporate surveillance, where workers can exchange experiences and tactics and build solidarity. By amplifying voices and mobilizing collective action, digital platforms transform individual grievances into potent movements for change.[19]

The transition to worker-to-worker unionism isn't just about adopting new tools or strategies; it's about reimagining the potential of unions in today's economy. It challenges the notion that unions are external entities and reinforces the idea that workers themselves can be powerful advocates for change within their workplaces. This model promotes a more democratic, inclusive approach to labor organization, which resonates strongly with workers disillusioned by traditional methods.

On Friday, November 17, 2023, employees of OpenAI, the creator of ChatGPT, threatened to resign unless the board stepped down and reinstated Sam Altman, who had been removed as the chief executive that day. Initially, five hundred employees of OpenAI signed a letter to the board expressing their loss of confidence and demanding the resignation of the entire board, as well as the reinstatement of Altman and his cofounder, Greg Brockman. As the day progressed, the number of protesting employees increased to about seven hundred, nearly encompassing the whole company. This marked an unusual incident of employee revolt in Silicon Valley. While not originating from organized labor, the employees at OpenAI demonstrated a unified front on issues they deemed crucial. It highlighted the significant influence that tech workers could have when they come together to address concerns within their workplace.[20]

If workers can unite over technological direction, one might wonder what prevents them from rallying together in favor of better wages and working conditions. Perhaps technology itself can provide a model; the relentless pursuit of innovation and rapid growth, while producing technological marvels, too often has overlooked the well-being of the workers who make it all possible. Elevating workers' well-being above the unrestrained quest for technological advancement and profits is not merely a call for better working conditions. It represents a fundamental reevaluation of priorities. Tech workers stand at a crossroads. They can continue to work for companies as individuals, lost in precarity and at the mercy of companies that take no responsibility for their training and well-being. Or they can realize their power and understand that, if the innovation that matters is one that improves lives collectively, success is a common endeavor, not something reserved for the talented and hardworking alone.[21]

Conclusion

Workers are told time and time again by economists, government officials, and businesses that the economies of the future will depend on high-skilled tech jobs. These jobs promise an improvement of the American labor market and a transformation of cities into "superstar cities," where wages and productivity will grow rapidly. But they also promise an improvement of work in general. Software developers who will design and build the next generation of digital technologies are just one subgroup of the tech workers who are portrayed as the talented workers of tomorrow earning the highest salaries; pursuing successful, stable careers; and being better equipped to navigate the challenges of the economies of the future.

Although the financial achievements of a few tech billionaires and the successful careers of a selected group of digital elites continue to form the dominant image in the popular imagination, the majority of software developers increasingly face precarious employment. The command of cutting-edge technical skills provides workers with little protection against flexible employment practices, exacting hiring requirements, and burgeoning temporary employment contracts that make achieving a stable career quite unlikely. At the same time, aggressive innovation is threatening the most vulnerable workers with obsolescence, forcing them to engage in an exhausting game of catch-up with rapidly changing technologies.

Job insecurity and precarious employment conditions are not confined to low-wage or gig economy workers. They also affect seemingly stable white-collar professionals, including software developers. Precarity is now distributed across all professions, affecting middle-class workers who were assumed to be safe due to their credentials and high salaries. They are not. Even the frontier workers who design ground-breaking technologies are no longer secure. However, this precarity is not evenly distributed.

What we see is that job insecurity impacts different groups in varied ways, often exacerbated by systemic inequalities. The pervasive image of the "ideal worker" in tech—typically young, white, and male and often a product of elite academic institutions—shapes not only hiring and promotion practices but also the day-to-day experiences and long-term career trajectories of those who do not fit this mold.

Workers perceived as ideal are better positioned to job-hop and negotiate higher salaries. They often find social closure in their managers, who are frequently of the same race and gender, creating networks that allow for greater mobility and more work opportunities. In the tech industry, it's not just about what you know; it's about who you know and what doors open for you. For women, people of color, and senior workers, these doors often remain shut, limiting their career advancement and reinforcing systemic inequalities. Precarity becomes much harder to deal with as a result of these inequalities, exacerbating the challenges faced by those who do not fit the ideal worker profile.

The inequalities of the tech industry contrast starkly with the laudatory accounts that assert that tech jobs open up new frontiers that will launch cities and nations into a more productive and equitable future society. But such promises are not new. In the 1960s and 1970s, a group of scholars that included Daniel Bell, Peter Drucker, and Alain Touraine prophesied the benefits associated with high-tech work. The emergence of new industries based on the production of high-tech goods and services would bring society to a new phase in which social problems would be eliminated through rational technological solutions. Central to their vision was the genesis of a "knowledge elite" who would preside over an efficient and meritocratic society. Workers within this emerging class would rely on intellectual rather than manual effort and master abstract scientific and technical knowledge that allowed them to manipulate information and produce high-tech goods and services. In the well-managed society of the future, highly skilled "knowledge workers" would emerge as a socially and politically dominant force that would not just fuel growth but spur the creation of a new just society.[1]

Although Bell and others correctly predicted the shift from manufacturing to an information-led and service-oriented economy, knowledge workers have not become the dominant class in society. They are not owners of capital; their intellectual capital is at the service of their employers. There is a critical difference between possessing that capital and controlling the production process. Software workers are smart, but they are still workers.

History teaches us that the disempowerment of previous generations of skilled workers should serve as a caution against the expectations we have connected to today's "elite" workers. The skilled workers of the precapitalist period—the masons, painters, and other specialists who occupied the vast guild system of the Middle Ages—were the "technical experts" and "knowledge elites" of their day, controlling a body of tacit embodied craft knowledge that was accumulated in communities of practice and passed down through formal apprenticeship programs. New craft techniques were the cutting-edge skills of the time, and the crafts played an important role in the international diffusion of knowledge. At the height of the guild system, the power of journeymen and master craftsmen was substantial, and their control over the "mysteries of the craft" was sufficient to guarantee a lifetime livelihood. However, the guild system and the power of craft workers were destroyed by choices that were made by other people who controlled production: choices for automation and standardized work methods that cast these craft workers into oblivion during the birth of industrial capitalism.[2]

In a similar way, the male secretaries, bookkeepers, clerical workers, and other white-collar office specialists, who grew in number during the early nineteenth century while enjoying prestigious and upwardly mobile positions, vanished at the turn of the twentieth century and were replaced by a low-paid, largely female workforce whose jobs were automated by typewriters, stenographic equipment, and adding machines. Stripped of the specialized, rarefied, or proprietary knowledge that had once given their work a measure of security and high social standing, clerical workers, like the craft workers before them, ceased to command high salaries and lost the power to negotiate the terms or conditions of their own employment.[3]

Just as in previous eras, today's software developers find themselves navigating an increasingly precarious labor market. They stand at the forefront of innovation yet face the aggressive policies of tech organizations and management that prioritize rapid technological advancement over individual job security and well-being. As automation, artificial intelligence, and the gig economy reshape the nature of work, software developers are becoming the modern equivalent of canaries in the coal mine: a warning sign of the potential risks and devaluation of skilled labor in the face of unchecked technological progress.

Despite the grim outlook that history presents, there is a beacon of hope: unity. By coming together and advocating for their rights, workers can influence the direction and ethos of the tech industry. Uniting provides them with the potential to foster an environment that values sustainable progress, workers' well-being, and democratization of decision-making processes. Collective effort could redefine the narrative, ensuring that technological advancement does not come at the expense of the workforce but is instead guided by the insights and welfare of those who contribute their skills and labor. In this future, in which workers have a say in their conditions and the trajectory of innovation, the industry can evolve into a space that honors human and technological progress equally. This united approach, where the miners take charge of the mine, offers a path forward that can mitigate the cycle of precarity and inequality, marking a new chapter in the relationship between labor and technology.

Methodological Appendix

Over the course of five years, from September 2018 to September 2023, I engaged in a comprehensive study involving interviews with 120 software developers based in New York City. The research began with a snowball sampling approach, where initial contacts led to further referrals. This method was particularly effective in the tech community, where personal networks and professional connections are strong. To broaden the scope of my study, I attended numerous tech meetups across the city, both free and paid. At each event, after obtaining permission from the organizers, I openly introduced my research objectives before engaging with potential respondents. This transparency fostered trust and often piqued interest among participants, leading to multiple follow-up interviews.

The interviews were semi-structured, designed to draw out workers' perceptions and experiences within small, medium-size, and large companies. By primarily using open-ended questions, I encouraged participants to shape their narratives, fostering a relaxed dialogue. This approach allowed for a deeper exploration of the lived experiences of software developers. I also prompted them to share specific examples from their daily work and notable workplace events, focusing on incidents they were comfortable discussing. These conversations, varying in length from forty-five minutes to two hours, were all digitally recorded and subsequently transcribed for thorough analysis while maintaining the confidentiality of each participant's identity.

A critical aspect of this research was the conduct of multiple follow-up interviews with the same participants over the study period. These repeated interviews were crucial for collecting longitudinal qualitative data, offering insights into how precarious work experiences evolved over time. This approach also highlighted trends and changes in the industry that may not have been apparent from a single interview. The longitudinal data gathered through the follow-up interviews were instrumental in tracing the trajectory of individual careers, as well as shifts in the broader tech environment.

In the initial stages, my recruitment of interview subjects at tech meetups predominantly led to interactions with young white and Asian male professionals, reflecting the majority demographic in software development. Recognizing the need for a diverse range of perspectives, I attended specific meetups and events that focused on the experiences of underrepresented groups in the industry. In addition, I reached out to online groups and forums organized specifically for women, people of color, and senior workers. These platforms proved instrumental in connecting with individuals who brought distinct and varied insights that were crucial to understanding the broader landscape of the industry.

Beyond the interviews, I immersed myself in the tech community by participating in hackathons, workshops, and conferences. This immersion allowed me to observe firsthand the dynamics of teamwork, competition, and innovation that characterize the industry. These events provided additional opportunities to engage with developers in less formal settings, often leading to candid conversations that enriched my understanding of their professional lives.

Throughout the study I maintained detailed field notes, capturing my reflections and observations. These notes were invaluable for triangulating data from different sources and identifying patterns and themes. I also engaged in regular peer debriefing sessions with colleagues to discuss emerging findings and ensure the rigor and credibility of my analysis.

The insights gained from this extensive research process not only shed light on the diverse experiences of software developers in New York City but also contributed to a broader understanding of the evolving nature of work in the tech industry. By integrating multiple methods and sources of data, this study provides a rich, nuanced portrait of an industry characterized by rapid change, innovation, and profound challenges.

Notes

Preface

1. All names of my interviewees and some identifying details have been changed to protect confidentiality.

2. Precarity, as discussed here, draws significantly on the work of Judith Butler (2004, 2009) who has expanded the understanding of the concept beyond the economic and labor dimensions. Butler's perspective on precarity or precariousness as a pervasive condition affecting various dimensions of life, including health care, housing, and social recognition, has inspired a broader and more nuanced view of this term. This dual focus highlights both the material and existential insecurities that shape the human condition in contemporary society.

3. While this research does incorporate an analysis of how race, gender, and age intersect with experiences of precarity among software developers, it does not extensively cover other potential intersections, such as sexuality, citizenship, or disability. This decision was made due to several factors, including the scope of the project, the accessibility of data, and the need to maintain a clear focus within the already complex fields of inquiry. While these aspects undoubtedly influence experiences of precarity and merit serious consideration, the chosen intersections of race, gender, and age are based on preliminary findings that suggested these were highly significant in shaping the specific professional vulnerabilities within the tech industry. Future research could beneficially expand to include these and other categories to provide a more comprehensive view of the dynamics at play.

Introduction

1. Age discrimination, nicknamed "the silent killer" in tech, is often omitted in critical analyses of the tech industry (Campbell, Gautschi, & Burley, 2019). Considered "too old" by thirty-six, software developers struggle to adapt to the sudden decline in their status. Unfortunately, workers' ages are not reported in employers' records, and little to no quantitative data are available on how employment numbers and wages relate to the age of employees. Nevertheless, a handful of industry surveys that ask workers their age paint a bleak picture. Stack Overflow (2020), a Q&A website for software professionals, found that the median age of a software developer in the United States is 33.7 years, compared with 41.9 years for the average American worker. Overall, the study found that 70 percent of software developers are younger than thirty-five, and only about 5 percent are fifty or older. Visier (2017) showed that tech companies hire a larger proportion of young tech workers and a smaller proportion of older tech workers than non-tech companies.

2. Autor (2019, 32).

3. Autor (2019). Salary data are based on U.S. Bureau of Labor Statistics (2023). Gayle McDowell (2011) delineates the enticing aspects of tech roles for young professionals, highlighting not only the competitive salaries but also the comprehensive range of benefits provided. These perks, which include remote work options, flexible hours, comprehensive health benefits, and generous parental leave, among others, make positions at tech companies highly coveted.

4. The sudden shift to working from home and the sudden demand for new technologies bolstered the power of the tech industry (Manjoo, 2022; Plagianos, 2021). The tech industry's most skilled workers—software developers—saw their value go up as their skills were urgently needed to help businesses transition to online platforms or help companies expand their digital infrastructure. In the first months of 2020, as the national unemployment rate soared to 14 percent, it declined for information technology (IT) professionals to 2.4 percent (National Foundation for American Policy, 2021). For many businesses, software developers became essential workers, and their jobs were even considered recession-proof (Streitfeld, 2021). While working from home, something with which IT professionals already had experience, software developers helped design and build the tools that allowed Americans, and the American economy, to survive the pandemic.

5. For a history of neoliberalism and relation to precarity, see Kalleberg (2009). On how IBM's innovative use of temporary workers in the 1970s to navigate fluctuating work demands laid the foundation for today's flexible labor models, see Hyman (2018). For an early analysis of how the software industry redefined the relationship between employer and employee by introducing project-by-project basis under short-term contracts, see Kanter (1995).

6. An example of the erosion of job security in high-tech industries can be seen in the recent practices of companies such as IBM and HP. Both of these tech giants have undergone significant restructuring and downsizing in recent years, often targeting their older and more experienced workforce under the guise of "workforce rebalancing" (Kunert, 2024). Similarly, Hewlett-Packard (now split into HP Inc. and Hewlett Packard Enterprise) has been involved in continuous restructuring since the early 2000s. In 2022, HP announced plans to cut up to 12 percent of its workforce by the end of 2025 as part of a broader effort to optimize operations and improve profitability. This move was part of a long-term trend at HP to shift away from traditional employment and toward a more flexible staffing model that relies heavily on contract and temporary positions.

7. Contingent labor accounts for 40–50 percent of the workers at most technology firms, which save $100,000 a year by using a contractor instead of a full-time employee (Wakabayashi, 2019b). In 2019, Google worked with 121,000 temps and contractors around the world, compared with 102,000 full-time employees, which is typical for the high-tech industry (Wakabayashi, 2019b). Temporary employees make less money, have different benefits plans, and have no paid vacation time in the United States (Sheng, 2018).

8. This instability was pronounced in February 2023, when many tech companies, having scaled up their operations during the COVID-19 pandemic's economic boom, suddenly shifted toward adopting leaner operational models. This abrupt change in direction reflects a broader industry trend toward cost cutting and efficiency optimization, underscoring the precarious nature of employment even among well-compensated tech professionals. For an overview of tech layoffs in 2023, see Inspirisys Solutions (2024).

9. For how white-collar workers internalize an entrepreneurial spirit as a way to cope with new forms of flexible work, see Neff (2012).

10. Throughout history, several programming languages have risen to prominence, only to be overshadowed by newer, more efficient, or more versatile languages as the industry's demands and focus shift. For instance, during the 1970s and 1980s, Fortran and COBOL were dominant in scientific computing and business applications, respectively. Professionals well versed in these languages were highly sought after, as their expertise directly correlated with the industry's needs. Mastery in COBOL, in particular, was considered a valuable merit, especially given its widespread use in the banking and finance sectors. Fast-forward to the twenty-first century, when the tech landscape witnessed the rapid ascent of languages such as Python and JavaScript. These languages cater to modern needs — web development, data analytics, AI, and more. Python, with its simplicity and versatility, became a darling for start-ups and tech giants alike. As these languages gained traction, the industry's needs changed. Suddenly, a software developer fluent in Python or adept at full-stack JavaScript development became more valuable, sidelining once crucial languages such as COBOL to niche corners.

11. See Albergotti and Matsakis (2023).

12. For an analysis of how precarious work has emerged as a contemporary concern among researchers, see Kalleberg (2009). For a recent expansion of the term to include high-status "affluent" tech workers, see Dorschel (2022). For a recent overview of inequality in high tech, see Neely, Sheehan, & Williams (2023).

13. This update on Standing's (2011) theory of the "precariat" is supported by recent discussions in the literature, such as those in Ross (2002), which explores how precarity permeates high-tech industries, transforming stable careers into contingent engagements.

14. According to industry reports and surveys, unmarried young white men continue to dominate the tech sector, constituting a substantial portion of the workforce. A study conducted in 2020 by the National Center for Women and Information Technology (DuBow & Wu, 2023) found that white individuals accounted for approximately 68 percent of the tech industry's workforce, while men constituted about 71 percent of the total tech workforce. Furthermore, diversity reports from major tech companies demonstrate the underrepresentation of women and racial minorities, particularly in software development roles (see, e.g., Google, 2023; Meta, 2022).

15. Factors such as race, class, gender, parental status, and age significantly affect individuals' ability to maintain professional status during transitions, make strategic career moves, and cope with unemployment. Mickey (2019) notes that initial public offering (IPO) transitions at start-ups disproportionately impact women with higher layoff vulnerability. Twine (2018) observes that referral networks often exclude Black women in tech, limiting their options for career advancement. Conversely, Shih (2006) finds that Asian immigrant engineers in Silicon Valley use job-hopping and networking to benefit from industry instability.

16. Bergen & Eidelson (2018).

17. *Fortune* (2018).

18. Elias (2023).

19. For visual data on how remote work since COVID-19 is exacerbating harm, see Marcotte (2023, 13–14).

20. The view of the high-tech industry as meritocratic is rooted in the ideas of the sociologist Daniel Bell. In his classic *The Coming of Post-Industrial Society*, Bell (1973) pronounced that the emerging "post-industrial society" is a meritocracy. Within this new society an "information economy" would arise, characterized by rapidly growing scientific and technical occupations that specialize in the creation and manipulation of information, as well as the development of technologically innovative products and services. The centrality of knowledge meant that educational attainment and training—and hard work—rather than race, gender, and class would determine individual success. "Knowledge work" would reward

individuals who possessed scientific and technical expertise with intellectually satisfying and well-paying positions and offer a pathway to social mobility.

21. Similar initiatives to the New York City Tech Talent Pipeline are found in various cities, each aiming to enhance diversity and opportunity in the tech sector. In San Francisco, the TechSF program focuses on training and employment services for underrepresented communities. Chicago's Tech Talent Pipeline is a city-led initiative to connect local residents with tech training and jobs, with an emphasis on diversity. Louisville's TechHire, part of a national effort, provides training and employment opportunities in tech for young people and underserved populations. Atlanta's Tech Bridge Program and Boston's Pathways to Tech are other examples that offer education, training, and job-placement assistance to bridge the gap between underserved communities and the tech industry.

22. See Thompson (2020) for a discussion on hacker culture and meritocracy.

23. As highlighted in Neff (2012), this emerging career model contrasts starkly with the traditional, hierarchical professional landscape.

24. Hoffman, Casnocha, & Yeh (2014, 24).

25. Hoffman, Casnocha, & Yeh (2014).

26. See Sheehan (2021, 2022) for an exploration of how dislocated tech workers enter a world of self-help career coaching that foregrounds self-improvement and discourages collective political action against employers.

27. Han (2018) defines precarity as the situation faced by individuals engaged in unstable contract work. In addition, this concept extends to a wider state of ontological precarity, exploring the diverse manifestations of vulnerability in life beyond the workplace.

Chapter 1

1. For how discussions about tech talent notably increased during the dot-com boom of the late 1990s and early 2000s, see Indergaard (2004); Kait & Weiss (2001). Focusing on New York City, they describe a period that saw rapid expansion of technology companies and a corresponding surge in demand for skilled technology workers, leading to increased usage of terms such as *tech talent* in industry discussions, recruitment efforts, and media coverage.

2. Zukin (2020) delves into the profound impact of demand for tech talent on urban economies, highlighting the "triple helix" of business, government, and universities. This alliance, bolstered by real estate developers and proponents of "academic capitalism," places cities in a dilemma: navigating the new economy's demands versus aspiring to community growth. This tension presents a significant challenge for those aiming to benefit from innovation. In addition, corporate and consultancy reports, such as Carlin, Gardner, Hancock, & Weddle (2019) and Frick, George, & Coffman (2021), emphasize tech talent's vital role in organizational success. These reports describe the intensifying global and

cross-industry competition for tech talent as a matter of survival, where the right talent is essential for a competitive advantage in an increasingly software- and technology-dependent world.

3. The confluence of military needs and technological innovation in the formation of Silicon Valley's tech talent pool is chronicled in Jacobsen (2015), which explores how the Department of Defense's quest for cutting-edge technologies underwrote the development of a tech workforce whose expertise became foundational to the region's global status as a hub of innovation. The historical narrative of Silicon Valley's rise and the Cold War's influence on the development of tech talent has largely overlooked the contributions of women and people of color. While pioneering white men predominantly occupied the tech industry, women's involvement in computing, as chronicled in Abbate (2012), and the vital contributions of African American women to NASA's space race, as recounted in Shetterly (2016), were significant yet underrecognized.

4. Green (1983).

5. Initially, in 1960, women constituted one in four computer programmers in the United States, a proportion that had increased to 35 percent by 1990 before experiencing a decline. By 2013, the percentage of women in programming roles had receded to 26 percent, falling below the 1960 levels. A parallel decline is evident in the realm of education, where women's share of undergraduate computer science degrees peaked at 37.1 percent in 1983, only to diminish to approximately 17 percent in the 2010s. These data, elucidated in DuBow & Wu (2023), underscore a concerning retrogression in gender diversity within the tech sphere, a phenomenon also analyzed in Ensmenger (2012) and Wajcman (1991), which suggests a complex interplay of social, cultural, and institutional factors that, over decades, have influenced women's roles and representation in technology and computing fields.

6. See McIlwain (2019, 2020) for a thorough examination of the failure of the Fort Rodman Experiment.

7. Wilson (1985); Wozniak (1984).

8. See O'Mara (2019) for a historical account of the role of race and gender in shaping Silicon Valley's workforce. Regarding racial dynamics, the 1970s saw marginal growth in Asian, Black, and Hispanic IT employment. However, Black and Latine workers did not get access to high-skilled IT jobs and instead congregated in lower-skilled occupations as computer operators and data-entry keyers found predominantly in government and manufacturing industries.

9. Although women made up 37 percent of computer science majors in 1983, managers privileged male hires (Massachusetts Institute of Technology, 1983).

10. For a history of hackers and the role of nerd and geek culture, see Levy (1984). For a critical feminist perspective on the same topic, see Thompson (2020).

11. See Ensmenger (2012) for a historical analysis on culture fit in the tech industry. The concept of the ideal worker is analyzed in Williams (2000), which

underscores the challenges faced by women and other underrepresented groups in conforming to the archetype of the ideal worker, who is typically envisioned as being fully available and entirely devoted to the workplace, often at the expense of personal life. This model, pervasive in the competitive and fast-paced tech sector, implicitly reinforces gendered and racialized norms by valuing overwork and availability above all else, thereby marginalizing those who cannot or choose not to fit this mold.

12. Cooper (2000) looks at how male tech workers perceived as "nerdy," due to their interests or demeanor, often find themselves at odds with these conventional masculine expectations. This discrepancy can lead to their social ostracization. In response, these individuals may seek to assert their masculinity through alternative avenues, such as dominating technical and intellectual domains within the tech industry. Consequently, what they refer to as "nerd masculinity" perpetuates a culture that values certain masculine traits over others, impacting the industry's efforts to achieve diversity and inclusivity.

13. Researchers agree that white, Asian American, and Asian men dominate the tech industry in the United States (Alegria, 2020; Han & Tomaskovic-Devey, 2022). Asian American men and women frequently experience racial/ethnic stereotypes (Chavez, 2021; Chow, 2023), as well as exploitation engendered by the H-1B visa system (Banerjee, 2006, 2022), and segregation into ethnic niches (Lee, 2013) forms persistent barriers that prevent Asians and Asian Americans from ascending to decision-making roles (Alegria, 2020; Chin, 2020).

14. For a thorough examination of the brogrammer concept, see Chang (2018); Losse (2012); Wu (2020).

15. Chang (2018).

16. Mickey (2018); Wu (2020).

17. See Levy (2014).

18. For an analysis of the pipeline myth, see Twine (2022, 65–69).

19. For a brief overview of discrimination in Silicon Valley, see Glaser & Molla (2017).

20. Shu (2017); Somerville (2017).

21. Conger (2021); Conger & Wakabayashi (2019).

22. Williams (2021).

23. For more information on age discrimination lawsuits, see Dorrian (2023); Kelly (2019).

24. DiBenedetto (2024).

25. For a discussion of ideal worker norms in the workplace, see Blair-Loy (2003); Davies & Frink (2014); Williams (2000).

26. Noble & Roberts (2019).

27. For a concept similar to the ideal tech worker, see Neely (2020), which introduces the term *portfolio ideal worker*. It describes how white-collar workers must continually invest in resources and development to create a portfolio of

skills and experiences. This portfolio enables them to navigate the turbulence of the neoliberal economy effectively.

28. See Alegria (2019) for an intersectional discussion of the glass escalator concept, which explores the obstacles that women—particularly, women of color—face in the tech industry regarding promotion and inclusion in engineering teams.

Chapter 2

1. ViGlobal (2018), an online career service for salary compensation and job matching, looked at seventy thousand résumés of software engineers and developers in 2018 and reported that the average tenure of an IT professional in the ten biggest tech companies is less than two years (1.76 years). In 2016, Hackerlife (2016), a job search engine for software engineers based in Vancouver, examined the public information of 2,766 software engineers (and related positions) across sixty-five companies in three major tech hubs across the United States (San Francisco, Silicon Valley, and New York City). Hackerlife's data rank those software engineers and developers by the length of their tenure at the firms. In San Francisco, software engineers tend to spend less time at medium-size companies than they do at large ones, although tenures at the latter can range anywhere from one-and-a-half years (in the case of Adobe, Uber, and Airbnb) to eight-and-a-half years (at Pixar). Other cities, such as New York, follow similar trends, with an average stay ranging from one-and-a-half to three years, with a greater tendency for workers to remain longer at large firms. For workers at small firms, and especially start-ups, the relative shortness of tenure reflects the turbulent environment in which those companies operate. Other reports include one issued by the software company DeepTalent (2016). After analyzing a LinkedIn sample of more than fifty thousand job profiles, it found similar short tenure lengths for software engineers and developers at large tech companies. For Facebook, Amazon, Google, and Microsoft, the median tenure length was only eleven, twelve, twelve, and twenty-four months, respectively. Such data show that even at the biggest tech companies, the average tenure for a software engineer is typically less than two years. Even at the most prestigious tech companies, workers are increasingly mobile and pursue short-term work "gigs" without necessarily being temporary workers or freelancers.

2. Sandberg (2013).

3. Mickey (2018).

4. The average salary for full-stack developers in 2024 remains one of the highest in the entire tech sector, with these professionals in New York City earning, on average, close to $134,574, with a $5,500 cash bonus per year. Since 2015, this role has seen a 35 percent growth rate every year in industries as vast as computer software, IT and services, internet, financial services, and higher education.

The report states that "the rapid pace of change in technology has made full-stack developers an asset to any company" (LinkedIn, 2020).

5. World Economic Forum (2019, 4).

6. Davenport & Patil (2012); World Economic Forum (2019).

7. Lane (2017) examines the rise of the "company of one" mentality, in which white-collar workers experiencing unemployment and job insecurity begin to see themselves as their own business entity, responsible for their personal branding, marketing, and continued professional development.

8. Cech (2022) critiques the widespread career advice that one should seek out and follow one's passion. Cech argues that the "passion principle"—the idea that work should be driven primarily by passion—is not merely an empowering career guide but a mechanism that can foster and exacerbate workplace inequalities. This principle, she suggests, privileges those who can afford to pursue their passion, often overlooking the economic and social constraints that many workers face. Cech discusses how the passion principle can lead to the undervaluation of necessary but less "glamorous" jobs, contributing to unequal pay and conditions that disproportionately affect marginalized groups. In addition, she explores how the focus on passion can lead workers to tolerate poor working conditions and exploitation under the guise of doing what they love, further entrenching disparities.

9. Thompson (2020).

10. National surveys show that meritocracy remains a strong moral ideal among Americans, who believe that economic success depends on meritocratic elements (Solt, Hu, Hudson, Song, & Yu, 2016) and, conversely, that poverty reflects individual deficiencies (Reynolds & Xian, 2014). The opinions underlying these ideals entail that those who "make it" are the hardest working, while those who don't make it are lazy and unmotivated.

Chapter 3

1. Stanworth (2000) discusses the dual effects of new technology on women's work lives. Stanworth points out the increased flexibility and potential for balancing work with personal responsibilities, which could benefit many women. However, she also addresses significant challenges, such as the risk of job displacement, the digital divide, and how new forms of work might reinforce traditional gender roles. The article further explores how these changes impact women's career trajectories, their representation in tech-oriented professions, and the quality of work available in the evolving digital economy. See also McIlwee & Robinson (1992), which analyzes how gender, power, and workplace culture intersect to create barriers that hinder the recruitment, retention, and advancement of women in engineering.

2. Wakabayashi (2019b) provides a compelling report on the scale of temporary contracts in tech.

3. Neff, Wissinger, & Zukin (2005) discusses how contract work in the design world is often perceived positively, being associated with increased autonomy, flexibility, and high status.

4. For women's representation in software testing, see QualiTest (2017); Zippia (2021).

5. Software testers are not valued as highly as software developers; they earn an average annual salary of $84,384, in contrast to $108,249 for software developers. For salary data, see Glassdoor (2022a, 2022b).

6. Although the turnover rate is difficult to distill into an industry-wide statistic, industry participants estimate that a tester's tenure lasts about three years, on average (Desyatnikov, 2019).

7. Surveys have shown that women's turnover rate in the tech industry is two years, while men's is four years (Moss, 2019).

8. Vu (2017).

9. Both profit and nonprofit initiatives launched in many of the nation's urban centers have encouraged women to enter the field of software development. In New York City, coding boot camps such as General Assembly; the Grace Hopper Academy, which admits only students who self-identify as women; and nonprofit organizations such as Girls Code and Break through Tech specifically target underrepresented groups and low-income City University of New York students.

Chapter 4

1. Kosoff (2018) explores the growing divide within companies, particularly at Google, between full-time employees and contract workers. Kosoff looks at how Silicon Valley has been pivotal in creating a new class of second-class laborers through flexible, contract-based work arrangements to maximize corporate profits while minimizing costs. The article highlights the distinct disparities in the treatment and benefits received by different categories of workers at Google, evidenced by color-coded badge systems. Contract workers, distinguished by red and green badges, while integral to the company's operations, are denied many of the perks and securities afforded to full-time employees with white badges. These contract workers perform various critical tasks but do not receive comparable benefits, leading to a segregated workforce within the same company.

2. The experience of isolation evokes W. E. B. Du Bois's concept of double consciousness, suggesting a parallel between the historical struggles for identity and recognition and the contemporary experiences of Black professionals in tech. According to a survey by the job search company Indeed (Gafner, 2023), 49 percent of Black employees express a desire to quit their jobs, driven by issues such as lack of pay transparency, a misalignment between their personal values and company values, and a lack of diverse leadership within organizations. Per Golden (2022), Black technology workers face barriers that lead to shorter job

tenures compared with their non-Black peers, with an average tenure of 3.5 years compared with 5.1 years for others. This trend is especially pronounced among those with less than ten years of experience. Challenges persist throughout their careers, including dissatisfaction with performance evaluations and pay equality. Racial pay inequity is evident, with Black job candidates experiencing lower wages and less frequent salary increases. Mid-career Black tech workers are promoted less often than their non-Black counterparts, and those with more than twenty years of experience often miss out on key career advancement opportunities. In addition, Black professionals face pressure to change aspects of their behavior or appearance at work. To address these disparities, employers must actively work on building diverse networks and improving inclusion practices.

3. Anderson (2023) explores the perceptions of racial and ethnic bias in hiring practices and performance evaluations across different racial groups in the United States. According to a survey conducted by the Pew Research Center in December 2022, a significant majority of Black Americans (64 percent) perceive bias in hiring as a major problem, a view that is more prevalent among Black Americans compared with Asian, Hispanic, and white Americans. This pattern is consistent in perceptions of bias in performance evaluations, as well. The article discusses the increasing reliance on AI by companies to address diversity and equity issues in hiring. While some believe that AI can help reduce human biases, others are skeptical, noting that AI systems can also reinforce existing prejudices due to biases in the data used to train them. The skepticism is particularly strong among Black Americans, 20 percent of whom fear that AI could worsen biases in hiring, compared with smaller percentages among other groups. This apprehension extends to the use of AI in performance evaluations, though to a lesser extent.

4. Tiku (2021) shows how, for years, recruiting departments at tech companies such as Google used a college ranking system to set budgets and priorities for hiring new engineers. Some schools, such as Stanford University and the Massachusetts Institute of Technology, were predictably in the "elite" category, while state schools and institutions that churn out thousands of engineering grads annually, such as Georgia Tech, were assigned to "tier 1" or "tier 2."

5. Alfrey & Twine (2017); Twine (2022).

6. Tiku (2021) discusses Google's recruiting practices at HBCUs and how these efforts may contribute to the underrepresentation of Black engineers in big tech. Tiku reveals that, while Google has engaged with HBCUs, the outcomes have not significantly boosted the presence of Black professionals in tech, partly due to various systemic and organizational challenges within these initiatives. Ehrenkranz (2016) explores the pervasive discrimination that minorities face in the tech industry, starting from the recruitment stage, highlighting how biased recruiting practices, including job descriptions and interview processes, can deter or disadvantage minority candidates even before they join a company. This dis-

crimination contributes to the lower numbers of minorities working in tech and affects their career trajectories and experiences in the workplace.

7. For a comprehensive list of tech layoffs in 2023 and 2024, see Stringer & Corrall (2024).

8. See Elias (2023) for how layoffs have disproportionately affected under-represented groups in tech, including cuts in HR departments and DEI initiatives. See Wingfield (2019) for research on Black health-care professionals that illustrates how institutions engage in "racial outsourcing." This practice compels Black employees to undertake additional, often unpaid, labor to make services more equitable and accessible for communities of color. Not only does this increase their workload, but it also exposes these employees to heightened racist attitudes and discussions, further exacerbating the challenges they face within their organizations.

9. The conditions described by my respondents are not unique to the tech sector and software development. Scholars have documented how Black and Latine professionals in both academia and architecture are pushed into less prestigious concentrations. For example, Kaplan (2006) finds that Black architects are less likely than their white colleagues to have access to opportunities for advancement, promotion, and upward mobility.

10. Kanter (1977) discusses a concept she terms *heightened visibility*, which refers to the increased scrutiny and pressure faced by individuals in roles where they are minorities. Wingfield (2013, 2019) builds on the concept by exploring the complex dynamics that shape racialized experiences in the white workplace. In addition, the prevalent stereotype that associates Black men with danger, lack of commitment, and lower economic status is critically examined in Feagin (1991), highlighting the persistent challenges and discrimination faced by this group in society and professional settings.

11. For an exploration of how Black workers navigate racial boundaries in the tech workplace, see Franklin (2022).

12. Evans & Rangarajan (2017) investigates the lack of transparency surrounding diversity statistics within Silicon Valley companies. Many of these tech giants are reluctant to share detailed diversity data, which could provide insights into the racial and gender disparities within their workforce. The reluctance to disclose this information often stems from concerns about public image and potential legal repercussions.

13. Birnbaum (2020) discusses how NDAs contribute to racial inequality in the tech industry. The article explores how NDAs often silence employees from speaking out about discrimination, thereby hindering transparency and accountability necessary for addressing systemic racial biases.

14. Miley (2019).

15. For the story of Palmer Luckey, see Feldman (2018). Other tech entrepreneurs in positions of leadership, such as Uber's former chief executive Travis

Kalanick, have ignored or enabled the racial and gender abuse taking place in their offices for many years. Kalanick was forced to resign as chief executive of Uber in 2017 after a series of racial discrimination and sexual harassment scandals broke out in the media, following a blog post about sexism in the company published by a female employee (Lopatto, 2020).

16. Scholars (Noble & Roberts, 2019) and industry participants (Toh, 2021) have challenged the tech industry's assertions of operating as a meritocracy. Ellen Pao, notable for her discrimination lawsuit against a prominent venture capital firm, has been a vocal critic of the industry's purported meritocratic principles.

17. Ray (2019) and Vallas (2003) explore the organizational structures and practices that influence racial dynamics within organizations.

Chapter 5

1. For the Zuckerberg quote, see Coker (2007). For a history of Facebook, see Levy (2020).

2. Carville (2019).

3. The tendency to lay off workers if they do not conform to management's new requirements can also be deduced from the industry's unusually high turnover rates, which show the number of departures divided by the average headcount in a given industry. Software-related tech companies had the highest turnover in 2017, with a rate of 13.2 percent (LinkedIn, 2018). Moreover, certain sectors within the software industry had even higher turnover rates—for example, the gaming (15.5 percent), internet (14.9 percent), and computer software (13.3 percent) industries (LinkedIn, 2018). The report also lists the specific occupations within the software industry that have the highest turnover rate: user experience (23.3 percent), data analyst (21.7 percent), and embedded software engineer (21.7 percent). It is in these industries and job roles that software and web development tools are constantly in flux.

4. Jiménez & Horowitz (2013).

Chapter 6

1. Harnett (2021) discusses the history and current state of unionization efforts within the tech industry. Initially, in the 1970s and 1990s, organizing efforts were led by underpaid women and people of color at semiconductor plants and later at software companies. The perception of tech workers as privileged and powerful, often portrayed by the media, contrasts with the reality that many face issues such as stagnant pay, temporary contracts, and little control over their work conditions. This stereotype has obscured the challenges faced by a large portion of the tech workforce not located in Silicon Valley but dispersed across various sectors nationwide.

2. Isaac (2019).

3. Team Blind (https://www.teamblind.com) is a networking platform designed to enhance workplace transparency, primarily focusing on salary transparency and other work-related issues. It enables employees to anonymously share and compare salary information, job reviews, and interview processes across different companies. This platform is particularly valued for its role in fostering open discussions about topics that are often considered sensitive or confidential in the workplace, helping workers make informed career decisions based on shared data from their peers.

4. Wakabayashi, Griffith, Tsang, & Conger (2018).

5. Frenkel (2018).

6. Twine (2022, 207–209).

7. Tarnoff (2018).

8. Tarnoff (2018).

9. For a news report on Kickstarter employees voting to unionize, see Conger & Scheiber (2020). For a news report on unionization at Alphabet/Google, see Conger (2021).

10. See Browning (2022).

11. See Alphabet Workers Union (2004); Berger (2024).

12. For more information on Amazon's hiring of Morgan Lewis, see Logan (2021). For more information on Google's hiring of IRI Consultants, who reportedly were involved in monitoring employees' discussions on internal forums and meetings, particularly focusing on identifying key organizers and union sympathizers, see Scheiber & Wakabayashi (2019).

13. Amazon has been reported to monitor workers' gatherings and to track unionization activities to preemptively address and disrupt organizing efforts (Green, 2023).

14. Ó Ríain (2004).

15. U.S. labor law currently does not have provisions to protect independent contractors, and its bargaining protections for subcontractors do not extend far (Hartmans, 2020).

16. Amazon (2024); Google (2024).

17. How affinity groups align with company culture can be seen at Google with its Employee Resource Groups (ERGs). Google's ERGs, such as Gayglers for LGBTQ+ employees and Women@Google, are integrated into the company's diversity and inclusion strategies. While these groups provide a platform for support and networking, they typically focus on professional development within the framework of Google's existing corporate structure. For instance, the Women@Google group organizes events and workshops that promote career advancement and leadership skills among female employees, adhering closely to Google's overall business and professional development objectives. ERGs are less

often engaged in advocating for policy changes that challenge the status quo of Google's operational policies.

18. Blanc (2024) argues that a worker-driven organizing model has the potential to successfully initiate numerous organizing drives, ultimately enabling workers to overcome the formidable anti-union barriers erected by tech billionaires. Blanc's assertions are grounded in extensive research, encompassing five hundred survey responses and over two hundred interviews conducted with worker organizers. The inspiration for this shift can be traced back to movements such as the 2018 West Virginia teachers' strike, which not only gained momentum through social media but also set a precedent that encouraged similar statewide actions across the United States, including in Arizona, Oklahoma, and Kentucky. These grassroots movements leverage broader socioeconomic trends—such as the glaring disparities engendered by neoliberal capitalism and an exceptionally tight labor market—that enhance workers' leverage and diminish fears of job loss.

19. Blanc (2024).

20. National Public Radio (2023).

21. The need for a more inclusive and comprehensive approach to unionization is also highlighted by recent scholarship on the tech industry. For example, Nantina Vgontzas's research on cross-supply chain organizing highlights the potential for shared precarity to foster solidarity across different sectors and roles within the tech industry. Vgontzas (2023) underscores the interconnectedness of various forms of labor within tech companies, from software developers to subcontracted janitors and food service staff. This cross-supply chain solidarity is crucial for building a unified front capable of challenging the systemic issues within the tech industry.

Conclusion

1. Bell (1973).

2. Belfanti (2004); Epstein (1998).

3. Greenbaum (2004).

References

Abbate, J. (2012). *Recoding Gender: Women's Changing Participation in Computing*. Cambridge, MA: MIT Press.

Albergotti, R., & Matsakis, L. (2023, January 27). "OpenAI Has Hired an Army of Contractors to Make Basic Coding Obsolete." *Semafor*. Retreived from https://www.semafor.com/article/01/27/2023/openai-has-hired-an-army-of-contractors-to-make-basic-coding-obsolete.

Alegria, S. (2019). "Escalator or Step Stool? Gendered Labor and Token Processes in Tech Work." *Gender and Society*, 33(5), 722–745.

Alegria, S. (2020). "What Do We Mean by Broadening Participation? Race, Inequality, and Diversity in Tech Work." *Sociological Compass*, 14(6), e12793.

Alfrey, L., & Twine, F. W. (2017). "Gender-Fluid Geek Girls: Negotiating Inequality Regimes in the Tech Industry." *Gender and Society*, 31(1), 28–50.

Alphabet Workers Union. (2024, February 29). "Google Lays Off Union Workers at YouTube Music" [Press release]. Retrieved from https://www.alphabetworkersunion.org/press/google-lays-off-union-workers-at-youtube-music.

Amazon. (2024). "Affinity Groups." AboutAmazon. Retrieved from https://www.aboutamazon.com/affinity-groups.

Anderson, M. (2023, April 20). "Most Americans Say Racial Bias Is a Problem in the Workplace. Can AI Help?" Pew Research Center. Retrieved from https://www.pewresearch.org/short-read/2023/04/20/most-americans-say-racial-bias-is-a-problem-in-the-workplace-can-ai-help.

Autor, D. H. (2019). "Work of the Past, Work of the Future." AEA Papers and Proceedings, 109, 1–32.

Banerjee, P. (2006). "Indian Information Technology Workers in the United States: The H-1B Visa, Flexible Production, and the Racialization of Labor." *Critical Sociology*, 32(2), 425–445.

Banerjee, P. (2022). *The Opportunity Trap: High-Skilled Workers, Indian Families, and the Failures of the Dependent Visa Program*. New York: New York University Press.

Belfanti, C. M. (2004). "Guilds, Patents, and the Circulation of Technical Knowledge: Northern Italy during the Early Modern Age." *Technology and Culture*, 45(3), 569–589.

Bell, D. (1973). *The Coming of Post-Industrial Society: A Venture in Social Forecasting*. New York: Basic.

Bergen, M., & Eidelson, J. (2018). "Inside Google's Shadow Workforce." *Bloomberg*. Retrieved from https://www.bloomberg.com/news/articles/2018-07-25/inside-google-s-shadow-workforce.

Berger, C. (2024, March 1). "Unionized Google Workers Learned Their Jobs Were over While Testifying to City Council about Why They Need Higher Pay." Yahoo Finance. Retrieved from https://finance.yahoo.com/news/unionized-google-workers-learned-jobs-210130626.html.

Birnbaum, E. (2020, July 1). "A Wall of Silence Holding Back Racial Progress in Tech: NDAs." Protocol. Retrieved from https://www.protocol.com/nda-racism-equality-diversity-tech.

Blair-Loy, M. (2003). *Competing Devotions: Career and Family among Women Executives*. Cambridge, MA: Harvard University Press.

Blanc, E. (2024, March 24). "Worker-to-Worker Unionism: A Model for Labor to Scale Up." Portside. Retrieved from https://portside.org/2024-03-24/worker-worker-unionism-model-labor-scale.

Browning, K. (2022, May 23). "Workers at an Activision Studio Vote to Unionize, a First for the Gaming Industry." *New York Times*. Retrieved from https://www.nytimes.com/2022/05/23/technology/activision-raven-union.html.

Butler, J. (2004). *Precarious Life: The Powers of Mourning and Violence*. London: Verso.

Butler, J. (2009). *Frames of War: When Is Life Grievable?* London: Verso.

Campbell, S., Gautschi, I., & Burley, B. (2019, October 30). "Ageism in Tech: The Silent Career Killer." Cascade Insights. Retrieved from https://www.cascadeinsights.com/ageism-in-tech-the-silent-career-killer.

Carlin, D., Gardner, N., Hancock, B., & Weddle, B. (2019). "Building the Tech Talent Pipeline." McKinsey and Company. Retrieved from https://www.mckinsey.com/capabilities/people-and-organizational-performance/our-insights/building-the-tech-talent-pipeline.

Carville, O. (2019, July 31). "IBM Fired as Many as 100,000 in Recent Years, Lawsuit Shows." *Bloomberg*. Retrieved from https://www.bloomberg.com/news

/articles/2019-07-31/ibm-fired-as-many-as-100-000-in-recent-years-court-case
-shows.

Cech, E. (2022). *The Problem with Passion: How Searching for Fulfillment at Work Fosters Inequality.* Princeton, NJ: Princeton University Press.

Chang, E. (2018). *Brotopia: Breaking Up the Boys' Club of Silicon Valley.* New York: Portfolio/Penguin.

Chavez, K. (2021). "Penalized for Personality: A Case Study of Asian-Origin Disadvantage at the Point of Hire." *Sociology of Race and Ethnicity,* 7, 2226–2246.

Chin, M. M. (2020). *Stuck: Why Asian Americans Don't Reach the Top of the Corporate Ladder.* New York: New York University Press.

Chow, T. Y. (2023). "Privileged but Not in Power: How Asian American Tech Workers Use Racial Strategies to Deflect and Confront Race and Racism." *Qualitative Sociology,* 46, 129–152.

Coker, M. (2007, March 26). "Startup Advice for Entrepreneurs from Y Combinator." VentureBeat. Retrieved from https://venturebeat.com/business/start-up
-advice-for-entrepreneurs-from-y-combinator-startup-school.

Conger, K. (2021, January 4). "Hundreds of Google Employees Unionize, Culminating Years of Activism." *New York Times.* Retrieved from https://www
.nytimes.com/2021/01/04/technology/google-employees-union.html.

Conger, K., & Scheiber, N. (2020, February 18). "Kickstarter Employees Vote to Unionize in a Big Step for Tech." *New York Times.* Retrieved from https://
www.nytimes.com/2020/02/18/technology/kickstarter-union.html.

Conger, K., & Wakabayashi, D. (2019, April 22). "Google Employees Say They Faced Retaliation after Organizing Walkout." *New York Times.* Retrieved from https://www.nytimes.com/2019/04/22/technology/google-walkout-employees-retaliation.html.

Cooper, M. (2000). "Being the 'Go-To Guy': Fatherhood, Masculinity, and the Organization of Work in Silicon Valley." *Qualitative Sociology,* 23, 379–405.

Davenport, T. H., & Patil, D. J. (2012). "Data Scientist: The Sexiest Job of the 21st Century." *Harvard Business Review.* Retrieved from https://hbr.org/2012/10
/data-scientist-the-sexiest-job-of-the-21st-century.

Davies, A. R., & Frink, B. D. (2014). "The Origins of the Ideal Worker: The Separation of Work and Home in the United States from the Market Revolution to 1950." *Work and Occupations,* 41(1), 18–39.

DeepTalent. (2016). "Tenure Length of Tech Titans Compared" [Blog post]. Retrieved from https://deeptalent.com/blog/tenure-length-tech-titans-compared.

Desyatnikov, R. (2019, July 24). "Why QA Testers Quit and How to Retain Top Performers." *Forbes.* Retrieved from https://www.forbes.com/sites
/forbestechcouncil/2019/07/24/why-qa-testers-quit-and-how-to-retain-top
-performers/?sh=56a9c7a861fc.

DiBenedetto, C. (2024). "AI Shows Clear Racial Bias When Used for Job Recruiting, New Tests Reveal." *Mashable.* Retrieved from https://mashable.com/article/openai-chatgpt-racial-bias-in-recruiting.

Dorrian, J. (2023). "IBM Settles with Eight Workers to End Age Discrimination Lawsuit." *Bloomberg Law.* Retrieved from https://news.bloomberglaw.com/litigation/ibm-settles-with-eight-workers-to-end-age-discrimination-lawsuit.

Dorschel, R. (2022). "Reconsidering Digital Labour: Bringing Tech Workers into the Debate." *New Technology, Work and Employment,* 37(2), 288–307.

DuBow, W., & Wu, Z. (2023). *NCWIT Scorecard: The Status of Women in Technology.* Boulder, CO: National Center for Women in Technology.

Ehrenkranz, M. (2016, October 13). "For Minorities in Tech, Workplace Discrimination Begins before They Even Arrive." *Mic.* Retrieved from https://www.mic.com/articles/156689/minorities-in-tech-discrimination-recruiting-best-practices-how-to-recruit-job-interview-tips.

Elias, J. (2023, December 22). "Tech Companies like Google and Meta Made Cuts to DEI Programs in 2023 after Big Promises in Prior Years." *CNBC.* Retrieved from https://www.cnbc.com/2023/12/22/google-meta-other-tech-giants-cut-dei-programs-in-2023.html.

Ensmenger, N. L. (2012). *The Computer Boys Take Over: Computers, Programmers, and the Politics of Technical Expertise.* Cambridge, MA: MIT Press.

Epstein, S. R. (1998). "Craft Guilds, Apprenticeship, and Technological Change in Preindustrial Europe." *Journal of Economic History,* 58(3), 684–713.

Evans, W., & Rangarajan, S. (2017). "Hidden Figures: How Silicon Valley Keeps Diversity Data Secret." *Reveal.* Retrieved from https://revealnews.org/article/hidden-figures-how-silicon-valley-keeps-diversity-data-secret.

Feagin, J. R. (1991). "The Continuing Significance of Race: Antiblack Discrimination in Public Places." *American Sociological Review,* 56(1), 101–116.

Feldman, B. (2018, November 12). "It Turns Out Palmer Luckey Was Fired for the Headache He Caused Facebook." *Intelligencer.* Retrieved from https://nymag.com/intelligencer/2018/11/it-turns-out-palmer-luckey-was-fired.html.

Fortune. (2018, July 25). "Inside Google's Shadow Workforce of Contract Laborers—Many Don't Have Health Insurance." Retrieved from https://fortune.com/2018/07/25/google-contract-workers-contractor-jobs.

Franklin, R. C. (2022). "Black Workers in Silicon Valley: Macro and Micro Boundaries." *Ethnic and Racial Studies,* 45(1), 69–89.

Frenkel, S. (2018, June 19). "Microsoft Employees Protest Work with ICE, as Tech Industry Mobilizes over Immigration." *New York Times.* Retrieved from https://www.nytimes.com/2018/06/19/technology/tech-companies-immigration-border.html.

Frick, J., George, K. C., & Coffman, J. (2021). "The Tech Talent War Is Global, Cross-Industry, and a Matter of Survival" [Report]. Bain and Company. Retrieved from https://www.bain.com/insights/tech-talent-war-tech-report-2021.

Gafner, J. (2023, May 18). "Report: 49% of Black Workers Are Considering Leaving Their Job and Here's Why." Indeed Career Guide. Retrieved from https://www.indeed.com/career-advice/news/black-workers-consider-leaving-job.

Glaser, A., & Molla, R. (2017, April 10). "A (Not-So) Brief History of Gender Discrimination Lawsuits in Silicon Valley." Recode. Retrieved from https://www.vox.com/2017/4/10/15246444/history-gender-timeline-discrimination-lawsuits-legal-silicon-valley-google-oracle.

Glassdoor. (2022a). "Salary: Software Engineer (April 2022)." Retrieved from https://www.glassdoor.com/Salaries/software-engineer-salary-SRCH_KO0,17.htm.

Glassdoor. (2022b). "Salary: Testers (April 2022)." Retrieved from https://www.glassdoor.com/Salaries/software-tester-salary-SRCH_KO0,15.htm.

Golden, R. (2022, February 8). "Black Tech Workers See Shorter Tenures than Their Peers, Report Says." HR Dive. Retrieved from https://www.hrdive.com/news/black-tech-workers-experience-shorter-average-tenures-than-their-peers-report-says/618475.

Google. (2023). "2023 Diversity Annual Report." Retrieved from https://about.google/belonging/diversity-annual-report/2023.

Google. (2024). "Employee Resource Group (ERG) Series." Careers on Air. Retrieved from https://careersonair.withgoogle.com/events/erg-series.

Green, K. (2023, December 5). "The Role of AI in Union Busting: How Employers Use Artificial Intelligence to Keep Workers from Unionizing" [Blog post]. UnionTrack. Retrieved from https://uniontrack.com/blog/union-busting.

Green, S. S. (1983). "Silicon Valley's Women Workers: A Theoretical Analysis of Sex-Segregation in the Electronics Industry Labor Market." In Nash, J., & Fernandez-Kelly, M. P. (Eds.), Women, Men, and the International Division of Labor (pp. 273–331). Albany: State University of New York Press.

Greenbaum, J. (2004). Windows on the Workplace. New York: Monthly Review.

Hackerlife. (2016). "How Long Do Tech Pros Stay in Their Jobs?" Retrieved from https://insights.dice.com/2016/07/08/how-long-do-tech-pros-stay-in-their-jobs.

Han, C. (2018). "Precarity, Precariousness, and Vulnerability." Annual Review of Anthropology, 47, 331–343.

Han, J., & Tomaskovic-Devey, D. (2022). "Is Tech Sector Diversity Improving?" [Report]. Center for Employment Equity, University of Massachusetts, Amherst. Retrieved from https://www.umass.edu/employmentequity/tech-sector-diversity-improving.

Harnett, S. (2021, June 2). "Tech Worker Organizing Is Nothing New . . . but Them Actually Forming Unions Is." KQED News. Retrieved from https://www.kqed.org/news/11874325/tech-worker-organizing-is-nothing-new-but-actually-forming-unions-is.

Hartmans, A. (2020, April 2). "'This Is Why People Are So Angry': Tech Giants like Google, Facebook, and Uber Built Their Empires on the Backs of Contractors." *Business Insider.* Retrieved from https://www.businessinsider.com/how-tech-relieson-contractors-temps-gig-workers-employees2020-1.

Hoffman, R., Casnocha, B., & Yeh, C. (2014). *The Alliance: Managing Talent in the Networked Age.* Boston: Harvard Business Review Press.

Hyman, L. (2018). *Temp: The Real Story of What Happened to Your Salary, Benefits, and Job Security.* New York: Penguin.

Indergaard, M. (2004). *Silicon Alley: The Rise and Fall of a New Media District.* New York: Taylor and Francis.

Inspirisys Solutions. (2024, March 5). "Tech Layoffs in 2023: Causes, Consequences and Affected Companies." LinkedIn. Retrieved from https://www.linkedin.com/pulse/tech-layoffs-2023-causes-consequences-affected-companies-inspirisys-bbc6c.

Isaac, M. (2019, October 28). "Dissent Erupts at Facebook over Hands-Off Stance on Political Ads." *New York Times.* Retrieved from https://www.nytimes.com/2019/10/28/technology/facebook-mark-zuckerberg-political-ads.html.

Jacobsen, A. (2015). *The Pentagon's Brain: An Uncensored History of DARPA, America's Top-Secret Military Research Agency.* New York: Little, Brown.

Jiménez, T. R., & Horowitz, A. L. (2013). "When White Is Just Alright: How Immigrants Redefine Achievement and Reconfigure the Ethnoracial Hierarchy." *American Sociological Review,* 78(5), 849–871.

Kait, C., & Weiss, S. (2002). *Digital Hustlers: Living Large and Falling Hard in Silicon Alley.* New York: Harper Trade.

Kalleberg, A. L. (2009). "Precarious Work, Insecure Workers: Employment Relations in Transition." *American Sociological Review,* 74(1), 1–22.

Kanter, R. M. (1977). *Men and Women of the Corporation.* New York: Basic.

Kanter, R. M. (1995). "Nice Work if You Can Get It: The Software Industry as a Model for Tomorrow's Jobs." *American Prospect,* (23), 52–58.

Kaplan, V. (2006). *Structural Inequality: Black Architects in the United States.* Lanham, MD: Rowman and Littlefield.

Kelly, J. (2019, July 23). "Google Settles Age Discrimination Lawsuit, Highlighting the Proliferation of Ageism in Hiring." *Forbes.* Retrieved from https://www.forbes.com/sites/jackkelly/2019/07/23/google-settles-age-discrimination-lawsuit-highlighting-the-proliferation-of-ageism-in-hiring/#70c776c05c67.

Kosoff, M. (2018, July 25). "Is Google's Caste System the Future of the Workforce?" *Vanity Fair.* Retrieved from https://www.vanityfair.com/news/2018/07/is-googles-caste-system-the-future-of-the-workforce.

Kunert, P. (2024, January 25). "IBM Talks Up Cost Savings, Including 'Workforce Rebalancing.'" The Register. Retrieved from https://www.theregister.com/2024/01/25/ibm_q4_earnings.

Lane, C. M. (2017). *A Company of One: Insecurity, Independence, and the New World of White-Collar Unemployment.* Ithaca, NY: Cornell University Press.

Lee, J. C. (2013). "Employment and Earnings in High-Tech Ethnic Niches." *Social Forces*, 91(4), 3747–3784.

Levy, K. (2014). "Yahoo's 2014 Diversity Numbers Show Workforce Mostly White, Male." *Business Insider*. Retrieved from https://www.businessinsider.com /yahoo-workplace-diversity-numbers-2014-6.

Levy, S. (1984). *Hackers: Heroes of the Computer Revolution*. Garden City, NY: Anchor.

Levy, S. (2020). *Facebook: The Inside Story*. London: Penguin.

LinkedIn. (2018). "These 3 Industries Have the Highest Talent Turnover Rates." Retrieved from https://business.linkedin.com/talent-solutions/blog/trends -and-research/2018/the-3-industries-with-the-highest-turnover-rates.

LinkedIn. (2020). "2020 Emerging Jobs Report." Retrieved from https://business .linkedin.com/content/dam/me/business/en-us/talent-solutions/emerging -jobs-report/Emerging_Jobs_Report_U.S._FINAL.pdf.

Logan, J. (2021, February 2). "12 Facts about Morgan Lewis, Amazon's Powerful Anti-Union Law Firm" [Blog post]. *LaborOnline*. Retrieved from https://lawcha.org/2021/02/02/12-facts-about-morgan-lewis-amazons-power ful-anti-union-law-firm.

Lopatto, E. (2020, February 19). "To Expose Sexism at Uber, Susan Fowler Blew Up Her Life." The Verge. Retrieved from https://www.theverge.com /2020/2/19/21142081/susan-fowler-uber-whistleblower-interview-silicon-valley -discrimination-harassment.

Losse, K. (2012). *The Boy Kings: A Journey into the Heart of the Social Network*. New York: Simon and Schuster.

Manjoo, F. (2022, February 16). "The Rise of Big Tech May Just Be Starting." *New York Times*. Retrieved from https://www.nytimes.com/2022/02/16/opin ion/big-tech-stock-market.html.

Marcotte, E. (2023). *You Deserve a Tech Union*. New York: A Book Apart.

Massachusetts Institute of Technology. (1983). "Barriers to Equality in Academia: Women in Computer Science at M.I.T." Retrieved from https:// logicmag.io/assets/pdfs/Women%20in%20Computer%20Science%20at%20 MIT.pdf.

McDowell, G. L. (2011). *The Google Resume: How to Prepare for a Career and Land a Job at Apple, Microsoft, Google, or any Top Tech Company*. Hoboken, NJ: Wiley.

McIlwain, C. D. (2019). *Black Software: The Internet and Racial Justice, from the Afronet to Black Lives Matter*. New York: Oxford University Press.

McIlwain, C. D. (2020). "The Fort Rodman Experiment." Commons. Retrieved from https://logicmag.io/commons/the-fort-rodman-experiment.

McIlwee, J. S., & Robinson, J. G. (1992). *Women in Engineering: Gender, Power, and Workplace Culture*. Albany: State University of New York Press.

Meta. (2022). "2022 Diversity Report." Retrieved from https://about.fb.com/news/2022/07/metas-diversity-report-2022.

Mickey, E. L. (2018). "Networks of Exclusion in a Gendered Organization in The High-Tech Industry." Ph.D. diss., Northeastern University, Boston.

Mickey, E. L. (2019). "When Gendered Logics Collide: Going Public and Restructuring in a High-Tech Organization." *Gender and Society*, 33(3), 4509–4533.

Miley, L. (2019, October 8). "Surviving and Thriving (While Black) in Tech" [Video]. YouTube. Retrieved from https://www.youtube.com/watch?v=7DaZbS-ilV0&ab_channel=Empovia%28formerlyChangeCatalyst%29.

Moss, J. (2019, May 11). "Disrupting the Tech Profession's Gender Gap." Society for Human Resource Management. Retrieved from https://www.shrm.org/hr-today/news/all-things-work/pages/disrupting-the-tech-profession-gender-gap.aspx.

National Foundation for American Policy. (2021). "Analysis of Employment Data for Computer Occupations." *NFAP Policy Brief*. Retrieved from https://nfap.com/wp-content/uploads/2021/03/Employment-Data-for-Computer-Occupations-From-January-2020-to-March-2021.NFAP-Policy-Brief.March-2021-1.pdf.

National Public Radio. (2023, November 20). "Hundreds of OpenAI Workers Threaten to Leave over CEO Sam Altman's Firing." All Things Considered. Retrieved from https://www.npr.org/2023/11/20/1214281184/hundreds-of-openai-workers-threaten-to-leave-over-ceo-sam-altmans-firing.

Neely, M. T. (2020). "The Portfolio Ideal Worker: Insecurity and Inequality in the New Economy." *Qualitative Sociology*, 43(2), 271–296.

Neely, M. T., Sheehan, P., & Williams, C. L. (2023). "Social Inequality in High Tech: How Gender, Race, and Ethnicity Structure the World's Most Powerful Industry." *Annual Review of Sociology*, 49, 319–338.

Neff, G. (2012). *Venture Labor: Work and the Burden of Risk in Innovative Industries*. Cambridge, MA: MIT Press.

Neff, G., Wissinger, E., & Zukin, S. (2005). "Entrepreneurial Labor among Cultural Producers: 'Cool' Jobs in 'Hot' Industries." *Social Semiotics*, 15(3), 307–334.

Noble, S., & Roberts, S. (2019). "Technological Elites, the Meritocracy, and Postracial Myths in Silicon Valley." In *Racism Postrace*. Report no. 6. Retrieved from https://escholarship.org/uc/item/7z3629nh.

O'Mara, M. P. (2019). *The Code: Silicon Valley and the Remaking of America*. New York: Penguin.

Ó Ríain, S. (2004). *The Politics of High-Tech Growth: Developmental Network States in the Global Economy*. Cambridge: Cambridge University Press.

Plagianos, I. (2021, May 2). "Tech Jobs Lead the Way in New York City's COVID-19 Pandemic Hiring." *Wall Street Journal*. Retrieved from https://www

.wsj.com/articles/tech-jobs-lead-the-way-in-new-york-citys-covid-19-pandem ic-hiring-11619956802.

QualiTest. (2017). "The Global State of Software Testers" [Report]. Retrieved from https://www.devopsdigest.com/the-global-state-of-software-testers.

Ray, V. (2019). "A Theory of Racialized Organizations." *American Sociological Review*, 84(1), 26–53.

Reynolds, J., & Xian, H. (2014). "Perceptions of Meritocracy in the Land of Opportunity." *Research in Social Stratification and Mobility*, 36, 121–137.

Ross, A. (2002). *No Collar: The Humane Workplace and Its Hidden Costs*. Philadelphia: Temple University Press.

Sandberg, S. (2013). *Lean In: Women, Work, and the Will to Lead*. New York: Knopf.

Scheiber, N., & Wakabayashi, D. (2019, November 20). "Google Hires Firm Known for Anti-Union Efforts." *New York Times*. Retrieved from https://www.nytimes.com/2019/11/20/technology/Google-union-consultant.html.

Sheehan, P. (2021). "Unemployment Experts: Governing the Job Search in the New Economy." *Work and Occupations*, 48(4), 470–497.

Sheehan, P. (2022). "The Paradox of Self-Help Expertise: How Unemployed Workers Become Professional Career Coaches." *American Journal of Sociology*, 127(4), 1151–1182.

Sheng, E. (2018, October 22). "Silicon Valley's Dirty Secret: Using a Shadow Workforce of Contract Employees to Drive Profits." CNBC. Retrieved from https://www.cnbc.com/2018/10/22/silicon-valley-using-contract-employees -to-drive-profits.html.

Shetterly, M. L. (2016). *Hidden Figures: The American Dream and the Untold Story of the Black Women Mathematicians Who Helped Win the Space Race*. New York: William Morrow.

Shih, J. (2006). "Circumventing Discrimination: Gender and Ethnic Strategies in Silicon Valley." *Gender and Society*, 20, 2177–2206.

Shu, C. (2017, October 26). "Three Engineers Sue Uber over Unequal Pay, Claiming Sex and Racial Discrimination." TechCrunch. Retrieved from https://techcrunch.com/2017/10/26/three-engineers-sue-uber-over-unequal -pay-claiming-sex-and-racial-discrimination.

Solt, F., Hu, Y., Hudson, K., Song, J., & Yu, D. E. (2016). "Economic Inequality and Belief in Meritocracy in the United States." *Research and Politics*, 3(4), 1–7.

Somerville, H. (2017, October 25). "Three Women Sue Uber in San Francisco Claiming Unequal Pay, Benefits." Reuters. Retrieved from https://www.reuters .com/article/us-uber-lawsuit/three-women-sue-uber-in-san-francisco-claim ing-unequal-pay-benefits-idUSKBN1CU2Z1.

Stack Overflow. (2020). "2020 Developer Survey" [Report]. Retrieved from https:// insights.stackoverflow.com/survey/2020.

Standing, G. (2011). *The Precariat: The New Dangerous Class*. London: Bloomsbury Academic.

Stanworth, C. (2000). "Women and Work in the Information Age." *Gender, Work and Organization*, 7(1), 20–32.

Streitfeld, D. (2021, July 23). "How Tech Won the Pandemic and Now May Never Lose." *New York Times*. Retrieved from https://www.nytimes.com/2021/07/23/technology/silicon-valleys-pandemic-profits.html.

Stringer, A., & Corrall, C. (2024, April 15). "A Comprehensive List of 2023 and 2024 Tech Layoffs: From Major Layoffs at Tesla, Amazon, and Microsoft to Small Fintech Startups and Apps." *TechCrunch*. Retrieved from https://techcrunch.com/2024/04/15/tech-layoffs-2023-list.

Tarnoff, B. (2018, April 11). "Coding and Coercion: An Interview with Björn Westergard and Will." *Jacobin*. Retrieved from https://jacobin.com/2018/04/lanetix-tech-workers-unionization-campaign-firing.

Thompson, C. (2020). *Coders: The Making of a New Tribe and the Remaking of the World*. London: Penguin.

Tiku, N. (2021, March 4). "Google's Approach to Historically Black Schools Helps Explain Why There Are Few Black Engineers in Big Tech." *Washington Post*. Retrieved from https://www.washingtonpost.com/technology/2021/03/04/google-hbcu-recruiting.

Toh, M. (2021, April 21). "Ellen Pao: Meritocracy in Tech Is a Myth." CNN. Retrieved from https://www.cnn.com/2021/04/21/tech/ellen-pao-anti-asian-hate-intl-hnk/index.html.

Twine, F. W. (2018). "Technology's Invisible Women: Black Geek Girls in Silicon Valley and the Failure of Diversity Initiatives." *International Journal of Critical Diversity Studies*, 1(1), 58–79.

Twine, F. W. (2022). *Geek Girls: Inequality and Opportunity in Silicon Valley*. New York: New York University Press.

U.S. Bureau of Labor Statistics. (2023). *U.S. Department of Labor, Occupational Outlook Handbook, Software Developers, Quality Assurance Analysts, and Testers*. Retrieved from https://www.bls.gov/ooh/computer-and-information-technology/software-developers.htm.

Vallas, S. P. (2003). "Rediscovering the Color Line within Work Organizations: The 'Knitting of Racial Groups' Revisited." *Work and Occupations*, 30(4), 379–400.

Vgontzas, N. (2023). "Toward Realignment: Big Tech, Organized Labor, and the Politics of the Future of Work." *Labor Studies Journal*, 48(3), 265–275.

ViGlobal. (2018). "Tech Industry Battles Highest Attrition Rate in the World—and It's Costly." Retrieved from https://www.viglobal.com/2018/06/13/tech-industry-battles-highest-attrition-rate-in-the-world-and-its-costly.

Visier. (2017). "The Truth about Ageism in the Tech Industry." Retrieved from https://www.visier.com/wp-content/uploads/2017/09/Visier-Insights-Ageism-InTech-Sept2017.pdf?mod=article_inline.

Vu, S. (2017, June 26). "Cracking the Code: Why Aren't More Women Majoring in Computer Science?" *UCLA Magazine*. Retrieved from https://newsroom.ucla.edu/stories/cracking-the-code:-why-aren-t-more-women-majoring-in-computer-science.

Wajcman, J. (1991). *Feminism Confronts Technology*. University Park: Pennsylvania State University Press.

Wakabayashi, D. (2019a, March 4). "Google Finds It's Underpaying Many Men as It Addresses Wage Equity." *New York Times*. Retrieved from https://www.nytimes.com/2019/03/04/technology/google-gender-pay-gap.html.

Wakabayashi, D. (2019b, May 28). "Google's Shadow Work Force: Temps Who Outnumber Full-Time Employees." *New York Times*. Retrieved from https://www.nytimes.com/2019/05/28/technology/google-temp-workers.html.

Wakabayashi, D., Griffith, E., Tsang, A., & Conger, K. (2018, November 1). "Google Walkout: Employees Stage Protest over Handling of Sexual Harassment." *New York Times*. Retrieved from https://www.nytimes.com/2018/11/01/technology/google-walkout-sexual-harassment.html.

Williams, B. A. (2021, May 25). "Did Tech Companies Keep Their Promises One Year after George Floyd's Death?" *Fast Company*. Retrieved from https://www.fastcompany.com/90640015/did-tech-companies-keep-their-promises-one-year-after-george-floyds-death.

Williams, J. (2000). *Unbending Gender: Why Family and Work Conflict and What to Do about It*. New York: Oxford University Press.

Wilson, J. W. (1985). *The New Venturers: Inside the High-Stakes World of Venture Capital*. Boston: Addison-Wesley.

Wingfield, A. H. (2013). *No More Invisible Man: Race and Gender in Men's Work*. Philadelphia: Temple University Press.

Wingfield, A. H. (2019). *Flatlining: Race, Work, and Health Care in the New Economy*. Berkeley: University of California Press.

World Economic Forum. (2019, July 2). "Data Science in the New Economy: A New Race for Talent in the Fourth Industrial Revolution" [Report]. Centre for the New Economy and Society, 1–21.

Wozniak, S. (1984). "Homebrew and How the Apple Came to Be." Atari Archives. Retrieved from https://www.atariarchives.org/deli/homebrew_and_how_the_apple.php.

Wu, T. (2020). "The Labour of Fun: Masculinities and the Organisation of Labour Games in a Modern Workplace." *New Technology, Work and Employment*, 35(3), 336–356.

Zippia. (2021). "Tester Statistics in the U.S." Retrieved from https://www.zippia.com/tester-jobs/demographics.

Zukin, S. (2020). *The Innovation Complex: Cities, Tech, and the New Economy*. New York: Oxford University Press.

Index

Max Papadantonakis is Assistant Professor of Sociology in the Department of Social Sciences and Global Studies at California State University, Monterey Bay.